W9-CYT-255

FLEECING GRANDMA
AND GRANDPA

FLEECING GRANDMA AND GRANDPA

Protecting Against Scams, Cons, and Frauds

Betty L. Alt and Sandra K. Wells

 PRAEGER

Westport, Connecticut
London

Library of Congress Cataloging-in-Publication Data

Alt, Betty L.
    Fleecing grandma and grandpa : protecting against scams, cons, and frauds /
Betty L. Alt and Sandra K. Wells.
        p. cm.
    Includes bibliographical references and index.
    ISBN 0–275–98179–7 (alk. paper)
    1. Older people—Crimes against—United States. 2. Fraud—United States. 3.
Swindlers and swindling—United States. I. Wells, Sandra, 1950– II. Title.
HV6250.4.A34A52 2004
362.88′0846′0973—dc22   2004054672

British Library Cataloguing in Publication Data is available.

Library of Congress Catalog Card Number: 2004054672
ISBN 0–275–98179–7

First published in 2004

Praeger Publishers, 88 Post Road West, Westport, CT 06881
An imprint of Greenwood Publishing Group, Inc.
www.praeger.com

Printed in the United States of America

The paper used in this book complies with the
Permanent Paper Standard issued by the National
Information Standards Organization (Z39.48–1984).

10 9 8 7 6 5 4 3 2 1

For Bob, Yvonne, Warren, and Rob

and for the two Colonels

Contents

Introduction

Flim-flam—a sly trick or deception; to trick or cheat
—*New World Dictionary*

* * *

C on artists are masters of manipulation. From the early Egyptian who added cement to his bread to make it weigh more, to the carnival barker shouting, "Step right up. See the three-headed woman," to the telemarketer convincing thousands that they have won a Canadian lottery, these cons feed off the gullibility and greed of one and all. Today con artists still lurk in the crowded cities and small towns of America spouting all kinds of ways to make easy money and continually gaining the public's confidence. The urge to get rich quick is so tempting that many people fail to see through the spiel of the charismatic con artist who knocks on their door, asks for help in a mall, sends a clever letter, calls on the telephone, or e-mails an enticing offer.

Although con artists prey upon "marks" (victims) of all ages, senior citizens—those individuals over age 65—appear to be particularly susceptible to many types of scams for a number of reasons. Many have accumulated savings or have excellent credit available, so they make ideal marks. They tend to be more trusting of others and therefore more gullible. They often live alone, are eager for companionship, and are more accessible because they are usually retired. Some are living on a small, fixed income and are enticed by the possibility of making extra cash or of saving money through "discount" offers for merchandise and home repairs. From the number of case histories appearing in newspapers and magazines and on television it appears that the words *elderly* and *easy mark* are almost synonymous. Numerous government and private agencies are concerned about financial fraud perpetrated against the elderly, and media reports indicate that this problem is "on the rise," "alarming," or "critical."

Statistics on the number of fraud occurrences directed against the elderly are difficult to locate, however, as there appears to be no systematic tally of incidents organized specifically by age. Speaking before the U.S. Senate Judiciary in July 1999, Susan Herman (Executive Director, National Center for Victims of Crime) did address the problem, stating that 20 percent of the elderly had been victims of some kind of fraud and that they were the most "underserved of any victim group." Statistics from the Bureau of Justice indicated that for people age 65 and over there were a million and a half property crimes in 2002, with a monetary loss over $1 billion. Unfortunately, the categories listed for property crimes in this statistic are household robbery and theft, which may or may not refer to scams. A 2004 bulletin from the American Association of Retired Persons (AARP) indicates that identity theft hit nearly 10 million Americans in 2003, but these figures are not broken down by age and probably include individuals of all ages. The Department of Justice *Consumer's Notebook* is more specific, indicating on the Internet in February 2004 that although those 65 and older constitute only 12 percent of the population, they make up 30 percent of scam victims. This statistic tends to support conclusions by the Department of Justice and the media that the elderly are disproportionately represented as victims of fraud.

Halting scams seems to be impossible. Repeated warnings from law enforcement agencies in newspapers and on television about those con artists perpetrating fraud either are not seen and heard, or are not taken seriously by the public. Many victims fail to report their losses to police due to embarrassment at their gullibility or, occasionally, fear of retaliation. The National Center for Victims of Crime indicates that the number one reason victims do not report a scam is that they feel the crime is a private or personal matter. In addition, apprehending the perpetrators is difficult because most quickly grab their spoils and vanish from the area. If law enforcement officials are notified of a scam, they are helpless to do much except to file a report and alert citizens to the possibility that scams are being perpetrated in their area.

In order to warn the elderly and their families to be more cautious, *Fleecing Grandma and Grandpa* presents in detail some of the major scams now being used by con artists, gives a brief mention of many others, and provides a few helpful hints to avoiding being flim-flammed. Also included are case histories from newspapers and magazines, the Internet, police reports, and telephone and personal interviews with numerous elderly individuals or their families, which illustrate how victims have been manipulated by con artists. Information was also gleaned from the few recent books that deal with this subject—books such as *The Art of the Steal* by Frank Abagnale, *The Big Con* by David Maurer, *Easy Prey* by Senator William S. Cohen, *Rip-Off* by Fay Faron, and *Crimes of Persuasion* by Les Henderson. The authors hope that reading this material will cause senior citizens to be wary of glib-talking strangers. However, with the huge number of baby boomers about to enter their golden years, unless these individuals become better able to avoid being fleeced, the next couple of decades should provide unlimited opportunities for con artists and horrendous headaches for law enforcement.

The authors would like to thank those who consented to give interviews or share their information. Thanks are also given to the authors' families; to Diana Johnson for her research help; to their agent, Mary Sue Seymour; and to their editor, Suzanne Staszak-Silva.

Chapter One

Misplaced Trust

---

* * *

Grant I may never prove so fond,
To trust man on his oath or bond.
—*King Lear*

* * *

Senior citizens are targeted because they tend to be trusting of others. Born in an earlier time, they are part of a culture in which a person's word was deemed as good as gold, and a handshake took the place of a contract. Believing in the honesty of their fellow humans, most elderly people are extremely gullible and simply do not expect to be cheated by those with whom they come in contact. Therefore, they respond readily to clever con artists and their many enticing spiels. In fact, a study released in 2002 by the Justice Department found that the elderly are "disproportionately affected by property crimes, including financial and consumer frauds" and that the frauds account for 90 percent of all crimes perpetrated against senior citizens.[1]

Con artists (cons) are masters of manipulation. They can successfully influence anyone to part with money or other valuables; these individuals, however, especially prey on the elderly person's trust and belief in honesty. Accomplished cons convince the senior citizens that they are genuine. As American Association of Retired Persons (AARP) board member W. Lee Hammond indicated in a Senate hearing on financial abuse and exploitation of the aged, those who perpetrate financial crimes against seniors project "an aura of trustworthiness . . . an appearance of reliability."[2] The adroit con artists tend to be polite, friendly, and even go so far as to make statements like, "I'd want my grandmother to have this" or "I know your family would want you to take advantage of this free deal." If all of these "nice" tactics fail, then fear and intimidation occasionally become the modus operandi. Usually these con artists are fast talkers, excited about their pitch, and are also able to get the gullible individuals excited. Urging the victims to make a quick decision, the trusting seniors take cons and whatever scheme (scam) they are working at face value.

The typical stereotype of a con is someone accosting a *mark* (victim) on the street or knocking on a door to offer some type of fantastic bargain, but scams are not perpetrated solely on a face-to-face basis. They come in the mail, on the telephone, on radio and television, and through the newspaper. For example, one ploy that appears repeatedly in newspapers and that entices many elderly people is the Work at Home scam that solicits individuals to work from their home and earn "quick money" after paying a "small investment." Basically the advertisements indicate that what is needed is someone to stuff printed flyers into envelopes for national merchandising outlets. There is the promise of big monetary returns with the individual doing only a few hours of work each week. This proposed type of employment is especially attractive to those elderly men and women who are homebound; the work at home offer, however, rarely results in any substantial income except for the cons.

Although a few of these job offers may be legitimate, most are fraudulent and require the "stuffer" to send money to purchase needed supplies or mailing lists to begin the job. The amounts of money requested can range from $40 to over $1,000. On NBC's *Nightly News*, an official of the Federal Trade Commission gave some advice regarding envelope stuffing, stating that "it was OK to stuff a turkey or a chicken, but stuffing envelopes usually did not result in a paycheck for anyone except the people running the advertisement." AARP indicates that this scam (which can be envelope stuffing, assembly or craft work, business opportunities, etc.) brings in $427 billion a year for con artists who pitch working at home as "a genuine opportunity! Guaranteed income!"[3]

This sounds very appealing, and one elderly man explained how he had been taken in to do envelope stuffing.

> I called on the ad and talked with a very nice man. When I called, I wasn't really thinking of taking the job. At first, he didn't think I could handle the job, but I convinced him. It was a good opportunity for me and with only a little investment. After I sent in the registration fee of $50 which was required, I received a bunch of advertisements—you know brochures—which I had to sort, fold, address, and stuff into envelopes. I had to buy the envelopes myself. Then I was told to send the stuffed envelopes back to the company, and if they met the standards of the company, I would be paid $1 for each envelope stuffed. How could I go wrong. I was home all day by myself and could easily stuff a box of 500 envelopes in a couple of hours. I thought I would be making a good amount of money for my work.
>
> Of course, I waited for my paycheck to come but it never did. Finally, I wrote to the man who I had talked with and was told that the envelopes I had stuffed did not meet the standards of the company—if a company ever existed. I never knew if there was a company, but if there was, I bet they sent out my stuffed envelopes. Naturally, I never received my expected $500 from the first batch I stuffed. I had spent the original $50, and the cost of the envelopes wasn't cheap. I'll tell you one thing. I've learned my lesson.

Unfortunately, this may not be true. Individuals who have been victims of a scam seem repeatedly to fall prey to these get rich quick schemes. Had this victim considered the situation more carefully, he would have realized if he could stuff 500 envelopes in a couple of hours and receive $500 for his work, he could, possibly, stuff four times that many in eight hours. This would net him $2,000 a day—an unrealistic expectation. But many people will take such offers at face value without considering the specifics. The con gets the victims excited about the projected monetary benefits, and they simply fail to make a wise choice.

The lure of easy money is usually too good for most persons to resist, and the types of con games out there just waiting for victims appear to be endless. Included among the many clever ways to separate marks from their funds are those confidence games known as short cons[4] or street cons. These tend to be the crimes of choice for many con artists, as they are simple to pull off and not a great deal of time is invested in the project. Also, even if the marks report the scheme to law enforcement officials, they usually are unable to provide a good description or other pertinent information about the perpetrators, so there is little chance of these men or women getting apprehended.

THE PIGEON DROP

An old, yet still often-used short con game is the Pigeon Drop. Although there are many variations, this scam is normally performed by two con artists and usually occurs at a public place—a mall, parking lot, or bus stop. A nicely dressed male or female con may approach the victim (the pigeon) and strike up a conversation. Shortly thereafter, another individual will appear and, after a few minutes, will indicate that there is a package on the ground. This person will inquire if the package belongs to either of the other two individuals. Eventually, the three look in the bag but discover no identification, only what appears to be bundles of money. The two cons immediately become ecstatic over the find. One says that they need to consult a lawyer who can tell them what to do with their newly found wealth. The trap has been set, and, as Eileen T. explained, she became a pigeon.

> I was at my car in the mall parking lot, and while I was putting my packages in the trunk a well-dressed young woman came up to me. She asked if I had dropped a small sack. I told her that I hadn't and we started talking, just general conversation about the mall and the weather. We introduced ourselves. Her name was Sheila. She was such a sweet person.
>
> While we were talking, another lady was walking by, and Sheila asked if the sack was hers. She, too, was a nice-looking woman, a little older than Sheila. This woman also didn't own the bag but asked if there was a sales slip in it that might have a name on it. When she looked in the sack, she became very excited. Inside the sack was $100 bills in packets. There must have been thousands of dollars in there.
>
> Both Sheila and I also got excited, and Sheila wanted to know who would put money in a paper bag. The woman said that she thought it might be drug money or something else illegal in nature. She thought that maybe no one would claim it, and we three could keep it. She said that she had heard of people finding money before and that there was a legal way to keep it.

Then Sheila said she knew a lawyer who could advise us. Wow! My mind was racing. My husband was ill, and we were living hand-to-mouth on a small pension. Some extra money would sure help, and this was a lot of money. Normally, I'm not greedy, but if this was drug money or a bad person's money, why not keep it?

Sheila said she would call her attorney friend, which she did. He told her that the law said that if we could each show him $3,000 cash to prove that we had sufficient funds to support ourselves during a period of 30 days while he tried to find the owner of the sack, we could keep it if no one came forward. I didn't have much money in savings, but I did have the $3,000. Amazingly, we all banked at the same bank. I drew out the $3,000, which only left $5 in my account.

I followed the other two outside, and we all put our money in those little white envelopes that you get in a bank and tucked them into the sack of money. Thinking back, since we used the little envelopes, I never did see their money. At any rate, we drove to the building where the attorney was, and the women told me that they trusted me to take the money into his office while Sheila went to the restroom and the other lady looked for a place to park her car. So, I went into the lawyer's office and waited. When Sheila and the other woman did not come in after a few minutes, I began to get nervous. I looked in the sack, and there was no money—only cut up paper. There wasn't any money left in the envelopes either.

I asked the secretary if Sheila had called to ask about lost money. The secretary informed me that the attorney was gone for the day and no calls had been received. What a fool I was. All my savings were gone. I didn't tell my husband, my kids, or the police what I had done. I was so devastated. I will never get over it. I've tried to figure out a way to make up for this lost money, but I haven't found a way yet.

LATIN LOTTO SCAM

Another variation of the Pigeon Drop is the Latin Lotto Scam, so named because this fraud is usually perpetrated in areas where there is a fairly large Latino (Hispanic) population, especially Latino immigrants. In New York City, for example, victims of this scam have lost over $96,000.[5] In western states, the current rash of these scams have been by Hispanics targeting Hispanics[6] as the following cases show.

Seventy-four-year-old Florinda Gonzales was at a Wal-Mart store around 10:00 A.M. when she was approached by a Hispanic female.

The female stated that she was from Costa Rica, did not speak English too well, and needed help interpreting the language so that she could cash her winning lotto tickets. Almost immediately a Hispanic male appeared and was told by the female con that the old woman had agreed to help them.

The male then stated that he was going to go to his home to pick up $10,000 to "put up front" in order to cash the ticket and dropped the two women off at a Wendy's. The victim did question why so much money was needed to cash the ticket and was told that this was because the two were not U.S. citizens.

When the man returned to Wendy's he made a call, allegedly to the Colorado Lottery Office, and told the victim they needed $10,000 up front to cash the ticket. If she would loan this amount, they would give back her money plus $2,500 for her help. Fortunately, the bank permitted the old woman to only draw $3,000 from her account, which she gave to the two con artists. After leaving the bank, she indicated that she wasn't feeling well and needed to get something to drink. The cons graciously took her to Taco Bell. Shortly thereafter, she went to the restroom, but when she came out, the cons were gone and so was her money.[7]

Another recent lotto scam that leaves one amazed at the gullibility (or greed) of some victims is that of a 69-year-old man who was told he would have to put up $25,000 because the cons with the winning lotto ticket had no identification.[8] Apparently, he never questioned why identification would be needed; he was only interested in being paid a big return on his money for helping the two men who held the ticket. This mark did not have the money requested but drove with the two men to his bank to apply for a $25,000 loan. Told it would take a fairly long time to process a loan application, he got a $5,200 advance on his credit cards. Because the victim could only supply part of the requested funds, the cons suggested that he add his two gold and diamond rings (worth approximately $4,000). Then he was given a bag of "money" to hold for safekeeping, waited patiently as the two con men went to call the lotto office, and, after examining the bag, discovered cut up bits of newspaper.[9] Eventually he called the police and told them he finally realized that he had been had.

A Denver couple lost most of their life savings in a similar operation. The husband went to a bank and withdrew the money Hispanic con artists asked him to provide. The perpetrators made an excuse to leave his sight and simply vanished. The victim explained later to reporters that he had hoped to make a quick profit.[10]

Although many might wonder how others could fall victim to such scams, cases like this are all too real. Of course, occasionally, a pigeon may become "a wise old owl" and not get caught in the usual trap. A man was approached in front of a Dollar Store by an elderly man who indicated that he spoke almost no English but had a winning lottery ticket that he couldn't claim because he needed to pay tax money on it. As is usual, another man came up and offered to call the lottery office to verify the needed tax. He spoke in Spanish, supposedly to a woman called Nancy who stated the ticket holder would need $3,500 in cash to pay the taxes. The pigeon felt something was suspicious, told the con artists that he didn't have that much money, went home, and then called the police.[11]

Another would-be victim reportedly scared off two potential scam artists who approached her and asked for $50 to pay an attorney. The woman stated that she couldn't help them, but the pair did convince her to drive them to the attorney's office, as they said they didn't have a vehicle. She wanted to be helpful, but after the pair were in her car, they began interrogating her about credit cards and whether she had a checking account. This canny senior citizen immediately pulled into the parking lot of a fast-food restaurant and told the two that she thought she was having a heart attack, whereupon they left the auto and quickly disappeared.[12]

Unfortunately, a pigeon failing to fall for the Pigeon Drop or Latin Lotto Scam is not the scenario that the police see very often. Most grifters are able to ensnare intended victims with no trouble at all and appear to always be one step ahead of their victims. If a mark should feel something is amiss and, for example, ask to see the "winning" lottery ticket, the con artists usually are quick to produce it. They have found the winning number of the previous day in the newspaper, have purchased a new ticket with that number, and show the mark that they, indeed, hold the winner. This looks good to the mark, and most never think to check to see if the number is old and no longer viable.

JAMAICAN SWITCH

Another short con, which is only a minor variation of the Pigeon Drop and the Latin Lotto Scam, is known as the Jamaican

Switch. Usually a man with a foreign accent, who supposedly can't read or write, is seeking a place to live and enlists the aid of the mark. Displaying a large wad of money, this con offers to pay for assistance and gets the mark on the hook. Almost immediately, a second man will approach and caution the foreigner to put the money in a bank. However, the foreigner indicates that he doesn't trust banks, but if the mark can make a withdrawal to show how easy it would be to get the money back out of the bank, he will make a deposit. Many times a mark falls for this ploy, withdraws money from his account, and hands it over to the con to show that the bank is actually an honest business. The con then says he will show the mark how to keep his money safe. He places the mark's funds in an envelope and puts it in his inside coat pocket. In doing this, the con switches the envelope for another stuffed with paper, hands this one back to the mark (who doesn't think to check it), and he and the other con quickly disappear.

The Pigeon Drop, Latin Lotto Scam, and Jamaican Switch are very effective short confidence games being practiced today as the perpetrators do not have to invest much time setting up the scam and can reap a quick profit. By the time the victims realize they have been duped, the con artists have their money and have safely moved to a new location. The pigeon is, literally, left holding the bag! For senior citizens, it is very difficult to recoup both their money and their self-esteem. They feel helpless and foolish and many times are easily duped by another scam in hopes of regaining a portion of their lost assets.

BANK EXAMINER SCAMS

The Bank Examiner Scam, usually practiced on older females, also gets its share of the unwary. Either in person with some sort of identification or by phone, a woman is contacted by someone claiming to be an official of the bank at which she has an account. The mark is given various excuses for the call: a survey is being taken, the woman's account has had some unusual recent withdrawals, there is a computer malfunction. The bank needs to verify certain information, as there seems to be a problem. Generally, the woman will provide her account balance and any recent activity. A few days later the phony bank examiner will call again, stating that the problem was the result of a dishonest teller stealing from customer accounts, including the victim's. To help catch the thief, the woman is requested to go to a specific teller, remove a set amount of money from her account, meet the official at a nearby location, and give the money to him for redeposit in her account. A receipt for the funds is provided by the official, and the customer is assured that the money will be returned to her account in just a few days—after the dishonest teller has been apprehended by the police.[13] Of course, neither the bank officer nor the victim's money is ever seen again.

An Independence, Missouri, man in his late 80s became just one of many victims of the Bank Examiner Scam when he was contacted by a man claiming to be "Lieutenant Kelly" from a police detective unit. Kelly presented the usual scenario about investigating theft by a bank employee and asked for the victim's assistance. The elderly man was instructed to withdraw $8,000 from his account as Kelly said he needed to check the money for fingerprints, and the cash was turned over to him in a parking lot near the bank. Three days later Kelly again contacted the senior citizen, told him that no usable fingerprints had been found, and asked for another $8,000. Two days after that the con artist requested another $1,000, which the mark obligingly provided.[14]

This particular scam works for a number of reasons. First, for some there is the thrill of being involved in a police case. One Bank Examiner con in Florida used the names Detective Davis and Detective Richardson from the State Attorney's and Sheriff's offices. Still another con artist carried a "U.S Agent" badge to impress his marks.[15] These false credentials convinced the victims of the cons artists' authenticity and made them eager to help the pseudo law officers.

Additional reasons the Bank Examiner Scam continues to be extremely successful is that victims become frightened that they will lose all of their money if they don't cooperate. Also, con artists may keep their victims so distracted that they are unable to think clearly and do not ask questions. Some victims have reported "they felt hypnotized as they became more and more involved."[16] None of the marks ever thought to verify that the bank official, detective, or agent was from a legitimate organization, and none seemed to realize that they might be involved in a scam until it was much too late to recover any funds.

ROCKS IN THE BOX

In use for decades, this scam still traps those wishing to get something for nothing. Usually the victims are approached by a con artist who offers to sell them a new TV, DVD, or similar appliance at an extremely low price. The victims may be shown one of the items in a box and can see that they will be getting a bargain. However, they are never permitted to take the item shown, as the con artist explains that they are getting a brand new one in a box never opened. After money changes hands and the happy buyers lug off their box, certain that they have made the best of the bargain, they find that they are stuck with a box full of junk or rocks used to simulate the weight of the desired appliance.

MELON DROP

Retired tourists are easy marks for this old scam as they, apparently, have the time and the funds necessary to travel. While sightseeing, someone will bump into the victims, drop and break an object—the melon—and claim it has a high value. Usually this individual demands compensation for the *victims'* carelessness. Threats of calling police may be mentioned. The melon may have cost the con artist only $1.49, but the victim might end up paying $50 or more simply to get the incident cleared up. Sometimes this type of fraud is used in restaurants, utilizing basically the same scenario. For example, a water-filled and diluted champagne bottle bearing an expensive label ends up broken. The mark is pushed into paying for the "expensive bottle" not realizing that it contained no champagne and was actually recovered empty from a dumpster behind the restaurant.

BAIL BOND SCAMS

In this case the mark usually will be phoned by the con artist, who claims to be a close friend of the mark's relative who has been arrested on a minor charge but must have bail money or spend the night in jail. This alleged friend asks the victim either to go to a bail bondsman for funds or to give the friend money to take care of the matter. For elderly victims, making the drive to the jail may be simply too stressful, so they are happy to have the friend come and pick up the necessary funds. In addition, many times the victims are so upset at the thought that someone close to them is in jail that they don't try to verify the caller's information. The victims discover too late that no relative was arrested; they have merely been fleeced.

WEDDING RING SCAM

This type of scam works well in restaurants, convenience stores, or gas stations. The con artists, usually a well-dressed and professional looking man and woman, either have a meal or make a purchase and then go to the restrooms and leave the premises. Shortly thereafter, they rush back, claiming to have lost a valuable piece of jewelry. Many times this is said to be the woman's wedding ring. She is distraught, and a big production is made of the sentimental value attached to the ring. Both employees and other patrons are encouraged to become involved in searching for the missing item. When the ring cannot be located, the cons tell the on-lookers that they will be staying a few days at a hotel nearby and will give a good-sized reward (let's say $800) to anyone finding the item.

During the search, an accomplice to the other two cons has entered the premises and hears the offer of a generous reward if the ring is found. After a short time the accomplice "finds" the item in the restroom, out by the gas pumps, or near the pay phone and exclaims loudly, "Hey, I found that lady's ring." Then the accomplice begins weeding out the marks with the story that he or she can't take the time necessary to return the item but certainly does not want to lose out on the reward. Generally, at least one of the other customers (the mark) will offer the accomplice an amount of money less than the reward ($500 for instance), hoping to make a profit when the ring is returned to its rightful and very grateful owner. The mark pays; the accomplice leaves; and when the mark goes to the hotel to claim the reward, neither of the con artists is registered there. The cons have made enough money to get them to their next destination (and next victims), and the mark is left trying to return a cheap piece of jewelry to nonexistent hotel guests. (Occasionally, this scheme is used in a mall parking lot, and the con artists indicate that they will be shopping in a particular store for a period of time.)

THE PYRAMID SCHEME (BINARY COMPENSATION PROGRAM)

This type of fraud involves a longer time commitment than the short cons. It was named after Charles Ponzi, who, in the 1920s, worked a scam to lure people into investing in a plan that guaranteed a high rate of return. Ponzi then used the money of later investors to pay off the earlier investors. Although he could skim money off the top, he could only keep the scam going for a short period of time before he ran out of new investors. From the Ponzi scheme one moves into the pyramid scheme where an endless stream of recruits is needed for success. Recruits give money to recruiters who, in turn, enlist fresh recruits to give them money. (Sometimes the envelope stuffing listed earlier becomes an illegal pyramid scheme if, on behalf of a company, individuals do not receive a service or a product but get instructions to place an advertisement asking people to send them money for information about working at home.[17])

There are many types of pyramid schemes—the original dinner party, Women Empowering Women, Friends Helping Friends, gifting clubs, and so forth. Reports of these scams have been on ABC's *World News Tonight* (November 1, 2002), NBC's *Nightly News with Tom Brokaw* (January 8, 2002), and CBS's *Sixty Minutes* (May 9, 1999). Of course, pyramid schemes don't just attract senior citizens. Many law enforcement officials, sports and entertainment figures, college students, homemakers, and those in business or government have fallen for these scams. However, the promise of high returns on their investments continues to lure the elderly on a small fixed income. One victim describes the consequences of investing in a pyramid scheme.

A friend of mine, James, who I had only known a short time, said he was investing in a club with other investors and that the profit on his investment had been terrific. He asked if I wanted to get in on this good deal. I don't have much money—just a small pension and some savings, but I invested $500. I really needed to make some extra money and didn't see any other way to do so. James told me I could tell some of my other friends about the deal, and I did. They also invested $500. I did get about $2500, which James said was only the beginning of what I could earn. It did seem to be quite a bit of profit so soon for such a small investment, but I was just glad to get the money. But it turned out there was no real club, and my new friend James was actually a swindler. Most of my other friends didn't see a cent of their money back. There was nothing we could do. The police told us James had set up a pyramid scheme and that the money I got back had really been a share from what my friends had put in. I guess James was always at the top. At least that was the way the police explained it. I felt like such a fool because I didn't truly understand what a pyramid scheme was. As part of the police investigation, I was required to give my $2,500 to the attorney general, and, of course, my friends pretty much dropped me after that.

Many individuals, especially women, are lured into participating in pyramid schemes when they are invited to attend dinner parties, are members of women's organizations, or become members of what are known as "gifting" clubs. As one woman explained,

I have played Bridge on Wednesday afternoons with a group of women for years. We are all very close friends. About six months ago Ruth (not her real name) started talking about investing some money and getting a lot of money in return. One day when we were playing and Ruth and I were at the same table, she started telling about this Friends Helping Friends investment plan. I started listening a little closer, and she explained all the details.

She told me that for a mere $2,000 I could "buy into" the club. She further explained that eight "volunteers" would enter the base level of the club, paying $2,000 in $100 bills. There were four "vice presidents" on the second level and two "presidents" on the third level with a CEO on the top.

When the eight volunteers (that would be me) paid their $2,000 or a total of $16,000 to the CEO, she would retire, and the rest of us would split into two new groups, and everyone would advance a level. I would eventually become a vice president, and then me and the other three vice presidents in my group would each get two new members to invest. The only thing I had to do besides recruit was to recite a statement saying that I was "gifting" the $2,000 to the CEO.

It sounded awfully good, too good actually, and I asked if it was legal as I certainly didn't want to get in trouble. Ruth said so, and she even said that there were not taxes to be paid because the money was a gift, so that when I reached the top and received my $16,000, I wouldn't have to worry about it with the IRS. They always say if it looks too good to be true, it is. They also say there's no fool like an old fool. Boy! I fell for it hook, line, and sinker.

Halfway to the top, before I could become CEO, someone official-looking came to my door and wanted to talk. I was told that this club *was illegal*, and I needed to identify who I had paid money to. I was also asked if I had received any money. I was shocked. I had been told by Ruth that this was not illegal. I had to pay a fine, and I know that a lot of the women had to pay back the money they received. It was really a low point in my life. I lost $2000 that I couldn't afford to lose. You're looking at an old fool who needed some extra money and thought she could get it the easy way.

It must be remembered that usually only the top of the pyramid or the organizer gets paid. Mathematically, it is impossible to continue a pyramid without running out of participants. Everyone is always told that everyone wins, but it has been calculated that 88 percent of those who participate will lose their money.[18]

So, why do people continue to fall for the pyramid gifting scam? There are several factors that cause this fraud to be so enticing to citizens, as Robert Fitzpatrick, coauthor of *False Profits*, explains.

- It appeals to basic American values as it is a giving organization, a share and support organization, which appeal to the elderly person.
- It is filled with lies that say it is legal and approved by authorities.
- People don't figure the mathematical impossibility.
- In America, people are told that all can succeed and, even if the profits from the scheme seem overwhelming, wealth can be achieved.
- Extra money is always needed as most people live beyond their means, and for the elderly, their income may be extremely limited.[19]

CHAIN LETTERS

This is nothing more than a get-rich-quick scheme (similar to the pyramid scam) that makes people believe, if they participate, that other people will be sending them scads of money. Follow the instructions and all will be well the letter recipients are told.

When the chain letter is received (via snail mail or e-mail), it will include names and addresses of people unknown to the victim. The receivers of the letters are instructed to send a minimum amount—usually $5 or $10—to the person at the top of the list. Then the victims are instructed to rewrite the letter, putting their names on the bottom, and eliminating the name of the person they have paid. Several copies of the rewritten letters are mailed, usually to relatives and friends, with the same instructions. Allegedly, the victims name will move to the top of the chain, and they will reap huge financial benefits.

Sometimes chain letters do not request money. Urban legends are popular forms of chain letters that are alleged to be true. They are transmitted from person to person via oral or written communication and always involve some combination of humiliating, humorous, terrifying, or supernatural events—which always happen to someone else. Sometimes, there may be a small threat, such as, "Behave yourself or bad things will happen."[20]

Urban legends tend to be hoaxes. Some offer free vacations, free money, free clothes, and free appliances. Others mention that women and children are dying in Afghanistan, someone in England or Australia is dying of cancer, or the National Kidney Foundation is asking for organ donations. Usually these legends want the receiver to forward them on to relatives, friends, coworkers, or other Internet patrons.[21] Individuals should never follow these requests, for even if they aren't asked to send any money, they may end up on another e-mail list and receive even more chain letters, some of which may request funds.

The issue with most chain letters is that it is illegal to request money and promise a substantial return to participants. It is considered a form of gambling and violates Title 18, U.S. Code, Section 1302 of the Postal Lottery Statutes.[22] As with the pyramid scheme, the idea that all participants will be winners is mathematically impossible. Also, consider that a dishonest originator of a chain letter could send out 1,000 letters asking for $5, with the originator's name always on the top. If only 700 people sent $5 to that top name, that individual would net a return of $3,500. Consider the even greater reward if a clever con mailed out the same number of letters for each of America's 50 states and received the same monetary response.

BUYERS CLUBS

Many people, and particularly elderly on fixed incomes, join Buyers Clubs because they wish to stretch their limited funds. These clubs usually promise great deals on products and services. Most are very reliable and do just what they promise; however, some consumers discover that while merely obtaining information about the club they have been charged for membership even if they never agreed to join. If offered a trial period or welcome package before joining the club and paying membership dues, consumers may unknowingly be charged for a membership when the free time ends. Also, they may find that the deals are not really as great as promised and that there may be hidden charges. Consumers should do some comparison-shopping to determine for themselves where the best prices and selections are.[23] Think twice about advertisements that promise products at incredibly cheap prices or "free," if the consumer pays for shipping. Many of these are designed to lure the unsuspecting into a buyers club membership.

PSYCHIC BABBLE

"Palm and tarot card reading by Olivia Dante," reads the small piece of paper tucked under an automobile windshield wiper. "She will tell you the past, present & future. She will guide you to Love, Happiness & Success. . . . She will call out the name of your enemies and reunite the separated. . . . Guaranteed results in 3 days."

Most people realize that psychic readings and related hoaxes are meant just to be fun, but many people actually have faith in what they are told. There are those who believe that there are individuals with special sight who can predict the future. Among them are many senior citizens who have lost a spouse, friend, or other relative and wish to commune with the dead or to learn what is in store for them in the future.

Fortune-telling can be a very lucrative business. Linda Malcolm,* who lives in Delray Beach, Florida, has made over $2 million in her career by charging people a mere $35 (to start with) to tell their fortune. One woman, Doris Hansen, believes that Malcolm is

* Names in this section have been changed.

actually a criminal who stole $300,000 from Hansen's husband Larry. When the 84-year-old Larry (who didn't die until age 87) met Malcolm, he had been told he only had 6 months to live. Malcolm was quick to explain to the frightened man that she was a Gypsy psychic and convinced Larry that she could cure his cancer. However, for her to do so would cost him a great deal of money. He was also warned that he couldn't tell anyone about the expense, not even his wife.

When Doris couldn't find the statement for the couple's emergency cash fund of $10,000, she became suspicious and went to the bank. The account was empty. She later learned that Larry had given all of their savings to Malcolm and had purchased a new Cadillac Escalade for her. "She told my husband she needed a truck to pray in for him," Doris said about the automobile purchase and added that Malcolm had taken away everything she had to live on.[24]

In another instance, Malcolm met with 55-year-old Marilyn Bates and her elderly parents. Bates had seen Malcolm's advertisement about her psychic powers and hoped she could help with some of the family's problems. Like Larry Hansen, Bates and her parents were sworn to secrecy and, over a period of time, gave Malcolm more than a million dollars.

According to Bates, Malcolm used a chicken egg to prove her psychic power. She broke an egg, a snake spilled out, and Malcolm told the Bates family that there was "still lots of evil around them." (Many times a Gypsy fortune-teller will ask clients to bring in an egg or a tomato. Then, when the clients are distracted, the egg or tomato is switched for another. When this new egg is broken or the tomato is cut, it will contain dead bugs, hair, or some other bits of debris. The clients are usually quite upset and will be told by the fortune-teller that this indicates they are unclean and will have to come back several times to ward off the evil.)

Because of the supposed evil around them, Bates and her parents were persuaded to continue keeping appointments. They believed what Malcolm told them because the psychic "presented herself very well."[25] (When Marilyn Bates finally told her husband that most of their money had been given to Malcolm, he divorced her.)

Bates, her elderly parents, Hansen, and 15 others have filed a civil suit against Malcolm, hoping to get some of their money returned. However, as Delray Beach Police Chief Larry Schroeder says, Malcolm may not have committed a crime at all. Malcolm certainly did not guarantee that Larry Hansen would be cured nor did she say she could cure Bates's life challenges. She didn't force these individuals to seek her out. She does make one interesting comment about all of the money she was able to get from her clients, "The money had to be cursed, because it brought me nothing but darkness."[26]

Another type of Gypsy fortune-telling dodge is *hakk'ni panki* (from which the term hanky-panky comes). After the marks have their fortunes told, the fortune-teller will mention to the customers that there is a spell that can double their money. Usually, the fortune-teller has the mark take out some money, wraps this in a handkerchief, and tells the mark to "dream on it." The next morning there is double the amount placed in the handkerchief because the fortune-teller has cleverly added money while distracting the client. Most marks falls for this trick and bring a much larger sum of money to the con artist, who again wraps it in a handkerchief while distracting the client and switching the money. This time, the victim is told to "dream on it [the money] for three weeks."[27] The mark does as told, but when the cloth is untied, finds only paper cut into the size of dollar bills. Meanwhile the fortune-teller has had time to move on to find another get-rich-quick sucker.

For those who seek psychics in order to commune with the dead, the scam is much the same. A woman in Virginia Beach, whose 83-year-old husband had died the previous year, made an appointment to see a fortune-teller or medium.

> I was told by a friend that Virginia Beach had really good "vibes" for those who were psychic. My friend also told me that she had received several messages from her late husband, so I made an appointment. I guess I had expected to see someone like the movie fortune-tellers—you know, long gown, lots of beads, a crystal ball. This woman was dressed just like me and lived in a typical house.
>
> At any rate, she gave her condolences over the death of my husband, asked a few questions, and just generally chatted. Then, she drank something from a glass and seemed to become sleepy. Finally, she said she had been able to see my husband and pretty much described him. I realize now that she could have described almost any old man and it would have fit how he looked when he got old.

But I was so wanting to believe that she could actually talk with him that I just kept making more trips to her home. After I had spent nearly $3000, I mentioned the matter to my son. He was very upset, told me I had been a fool and pointed out how the woman kept me coming back to see her. He was right; I could see how she had tricked me, but I so wanted to believe her, to have what she told me be true.

Fortune-tellers are able to deceive individuals because they are clever and listen closely to what is being said by the client. Chatting with individuals for a few minutes before beginning a session or a reading can help them glean a great deal of information that can be used later as messages from the dead and put the client in a suitable frame of mind. Sometimes a fortune-teller will have another "client" waiting in an outer room. This individual (who is actually a decoy of the fortune-teller) will begin a conversation with the real client. During this conversation, the employee will glean bits of information that can be given to the fortune-teller before the scheduled reading starts. Standard phrases such as, "I can tell you loved your husband/wife very much," or "I can tell your husband/wife wishes to speak with you," or "Your husband/wife is happy and wishes you to be happy also," consoles those who are left behind and lulls them into returning for more messages. For those seeking information about their future, the fortune-teller's confirmation that they will have a long, happy life nearly always brings the desired return visit—and additional payments.

This type of psychic scam draws customers from all walks of life, is still practiced across the country, and provides a good source of income for the practitioner. Again, it must be emphasized that the practice of telling fortunes is not illegal; however, it is difficult to understand how anyone would fall for this type of ruse.

PET SCAMS

Even having a pet sometimes can put one at risk to be conned. An elderly woman living in a small town in California explained this best.

One day my cat was missing, and I placed an ad in the paper and put up posters around the neighborhood. I also let the animal shelter, veterinarians, and pet hospitals know about Fluffy. A few days later I accepted a collect call from someone who claimed to be working for a furniture moving firm and who claimed he had found a cat in the company's van. At the time this man and his helper were several states away but would be driving back to my area.

The mover asked for a description of the cat, and when I gave it to him, he said he was certain it was my cat. I was a little suspicious so I asked how they had gotten my phone number, and the man explained that he had called one of the animal shelters after he and his helper had figured out what city the cat might have come from. This sounded plausible.

The movers wanted me to wire money to them so they could afford to bring Fluffy home. I was a little uncomfortable with this proposition, but I loved Fluffy so much that I wanted it to be true that she was found. So I wired the movers $300, even though I felt uneasy about doing so, and the movers would not answer many of my questions and seemed evasive. I guess I did it because I loved that cat. I waited for the movers to arrive back in town, but I never heard from them again. A few days later Fluffy came home on her own!

Frequently, however, the money is gone and the pet does not return. In fact, money can be made by stealing pets (particularly pedigreed dogs) and then calling the owners to get money up front in order to make a trip to return the pet. Sometimes the pet *is* returned; many times this is just another scam.

PROTECTING THE PUBLIC

Senator John Breaux of Louisiana and the Special Committee on Aging have indicated that 30 percent of all crimes against the elderly involve financial abuse and that there may be as many as four times as many cases of elder financial abuse that go unreported—three to five million seniors annually.[28] On February 10, 2003, Senator John Breaux, Ranking Member, Senate Special Committee on Aging (along with Senator Orrin Hatch) introduced in the Senate the Elder Justice Act of 2003. If passed, among other things, the new law would:

- Establish dual Office of Elder Justice in the Department of Health and Human Services/Administration on Aging and

Department of Justice to coordinate elder abuse prevention efforts nationally.

- Require an FBI criminal background check of long-term care aides.
- Establish an Office of Adult Protective Services within the Department of Health and Human Services' Administration for Children and Families agency.
- Enhance law enforcement response.[29]

The Breaux act is a very important step toward helping to ensure the financial safety of vulnerable elders and should aid law enforcement officials who are eager to protect the public against fraud. However, because law enforcement often does not learn of the scam until it is too late for the victims, the public needs to be aware of what they can do to prevent falling prey to crafty con artists.

- Don't believe any story about sharing accidentally found money. Tell the con artist who found the money to take it to the nearest police department.
- Never give money to a stranger.
- Contact the police immediately if you suspect a scam. (In the case of the "wise old owl" who didn't get caught in the Pigeon Drop, he should not have waited until he got home to notify police.)
- Closely observe strangers who approach with interesting offers. In this way an individual can provide accurate descriptions (including the stranger's clothing, hair color, eye color, height, race or ethnicity, car license, etc.) so that the con artists may be stopped before swindling the next victim.[30]

In the case of lotto scams, chain letters, and pyramid schemes, the best advice that can be given is to question investments that provide big financial gains too easily. For some of the other short cons, be aware that the con artist is lurking out there, just waiting to trap the gullible and greedy.

Of course, some people will always become victims. To try and protect senior citizens from joining this number, most states have introduced laws to help prosecute people who steal from the elderly.

These statutes usually consider those over 60 as elderly, and there are usually somewhat stiffer penalties applied to those who separate the elderly from their assets. Still, as can be seen in this and following chapters, not all cases are charged as a crime for a number of reasons: They aren't reported; there isn't adequate identification of the perpetrator; cons move frequently; and technically, the con may not be illegal.

Chapter Two

I'm Safe at Home . . . Aren't I?

* * *

A fool and his money are soon parted.
—English proverb

* * *

The elderly can become victims of adroit con artists in their own homes. Losses from scams connected with property are frequent and can run from small amounts to thousands of dollars. Also, nearly half of the attempts at fraud (including homeowner fraud) listed in a National Crime Victimization Survey were successful.[1]

Consider the case of Mrs. Jensen, a 78-year-old widow who lived alone. One afternoon while she was watching television, the doorbell rang, and on her front porch was a polite young man. He stated that he had finished roofing a house down the street and while driving by her home he noticed that she had some loose shingles. He further indicated that he had purchased too many shingles for a previous job and would be happy to reroof her house for $2000.

Studies show that Mrs. Jensen was the perfect mark. She lived alone, knew that her roof was in disrepair from the previous winter's storms, and didn't wish to bother her son about the problem as he was busy with his job and family. Like many victims of fraud, she knew nothing about the cost of roof repair nor did she make any attempt to investigate the credentials of the man at her door before taking the bait.[2] She merely agreed to the offer and asked when the job would be completed. The roofer stated that he would need to buy a few more shingles and asked for the $2000 in advance to make the purchase. Although seniors are constantly being warned not to judge a nice young man's integrity by how he sounds,[3] without hesitating, Mrs. Jensen gave the man the required money and never saw him again. She became a victim of advance fee fraud.

Thousands of such unscrupulous transactions occur every month across the United States. As 79-year-old Robert K., who also was the victim of a roofing scam recently, said, "You've got to be able to trust people. How can people live if they always have to be suspicious of everyone they meet? But I guess I've just been too trusting. I'm gonna have to learn to watch out for people."

Local con artists cruise neighborhoods looking for just such unsuspecting or trusting marks like Mrs. Jensen and Robert K. These grifters usually insist on an immediate answer, want money up front, and certainly do not wish to be confronted by a potential victim's family members. The scams work because, once again, when the victims discover their mistake, they are too ashamed to tell their families or law enforcement officials.[4] Of course, there are always people who are simply greedy and are taken as they try to get something for nothing. Also, it appears that people are much more hesitant to say no when approached face-to-face than if they can decline without having personal contact.[5] Whatever the reason, the con artist is home free and simply moves on to the next prey with the same scam, or with one of many others that have been conceived to target the unwary homeowner.

DOOR-TO-DOOR CONTACTS

Although many door-to-door sales pitches are completely reputable and furnish the products or services promised, many do not. One of the most common types of scams is that of asphalt paving. Law enforcement personnel often warn the public that a particular area is "experiencing a rash of home repair scams"[6] as con artists move around the country. Police departments sometimes refer to these traveling groups as "Gypsies," "vagabond thieves," "Romany nomads," or "Irish travelers." Driving new vehicles with

realistic-looking paving equipment and wearing workmen's clothing, they cruise around town looking for homes with asphalt
driveways.[7] Similar to the roofing scam, the cons announce that
they have been paving a new subdivision or the parking lot of a
new mall and noticed that the victim's driveway certainly needed
refinishing. They would be glad to do it for half the price a local
paver would charge because they have extra asphalt in their mixer.
However, a quick decision is required, as the asphalt needs to be
applied immediately.

Usually friendly and courteous, the would-be pavers point out
that the look of the property will be greatly improved or that the
value of the home will be increased when the driveway is resur-
faced. "They seemed genuinely concerned with helping me keep
my property in good shape," one elderly woman explained. "The
drive hadn't been fixed since before my husband died 7 years ago
and was just full of cracks. It did help the place's appearance—for
a few days." Certainly it was only a few days before the newly
applied, shiny surface began to break apart and dissolve with the
spring rain, as it was just a light coating of oil. Only then did the
woman realize that she had become a victim.

One of two elderly sisters, Elsie also became an asphalt-paver
victim. Sitting in the living room of her sister Margaret's small
brick home and providing steaming cups of coffee during an
interview, Elsie explained that a man had first approached Margaret about a "deal on paving her driveway as the old asphalt had
begun to crack." Margaret did not have money necessary for the
job, but she told the man that Elsie's home might need the product. Elsie knew that her driveway was in bad repair, decided to
have the job done, and gave the paver an advance fee of $700 in
cash and a check for $400. The man promised to be back the next
day and deliver the asphalt. However, 3 days passed and no one
showed up. About a week later Elsie returned home from an
errand, and in her driveway was a huge pile of cold asphalt.
Although she reported this to the police, technically there was no
crime. Elsie *assumed* the man would resurface her driveway; all he
had promised was to deliver asphalt, which he had done. No written contract had been made, Elsie had paid before seeing the work
completed, and she could only describe to police that the man was
"tall and with dark hair." Elsie was caught. She had no recourse

except to spend additional money to hire someone to cart away the pile of paving.

Sometimes, but only occasionally, a victim is saved. An elderly couple living in a rural area were approached by a Gypsy paver (sometimes called Irish travelers or Romany nomads) who wanted $12,000 to resurface their extensive drive and parking area. Because he was so friendly, the couple invited him in for coffee. While in their home he spotted a collection of antique clocks that had belonged to the old man's grandfather. The paver offered to discount the job by several thousand dollars in exchange for several of the clocks. An agreement was reached whereby the couple gave him the clocks plus a check for $10,000, although the woman indicated that she would have to call her broker and have funds transferred to cover that amount. She asked for a phone number where he could be reached and, after some hesitation, the paver provided her with an 800 number.

After the paver had departed, the woman called her stockbroker and asked him to transfer $10,000 into her checking account. When he questioned her about the transaction, she explained that she was having repair work done on the couple's home. Becoming suspicious, the alert broker questioned her further and indicated that he felt this was a scam. He checked on paving prices, discovered $10,000 was completely out of line, called law enforcement officials, and had her stop payment on the couple's check. When the paver was contacted through the 800 phone number by a police officer, he refused to give his name and location. Upon checking a few days later, the police discovered that the 800 number was no longer in service, and a fictitious name had been used to register it. Fortunately for this couple, the quick thinking of their broker meant that they did not lose their money—only the antique clocks.

Unlike this case, the Gypsy pavers usually reap untold profit from numerous townspeople and are gone before police are aware of their presence. Publications such as those below warning residents of paving scams appear in local newspapers and are published by Better Business associations in many towns. In November 2001, one daily newspaper reported that the district attorney's office was warning the public about an upturn in the number of consumer fraud complaints. A tip sheet from that agency and the Better Business Bureau (BBB) advised consumers to:

- Never pay for services in advance and never pay with cash.
- Get a receipt with detailed information about the person or business.
- Do not sign any agreement you don't understand, and always get a contract.
- Do not leave any blank spaces in a written agreement.
- Do not sign a blank agreement. (Many elderly do this as they either have eye problems or, in cases with recent immigrants, can't read English well enough to understand the document.)
- Check with the local BBB or the district attorney's office to know if any complaints have been filed against a business or individual.
- Perform independent research on a company's history.[8]

However, by the time these warnings were published, the pavers were traveling to another community or another state in search of more unsuspecting victims and were home free.

Of course, roofers and pavers are not the only door-to-door frauds perpetrated on the elderly. The Texas Crime Prevention Association warns the elderly that tree trimmers, house painters, or other contractors roam neighborhoods selecting targets. Stating that they are a "local business," they offer their services for up-front money, usually at a minimum of half the regular total cost.[9] The marks are lured into a false sense of security, assuming that if the work is not satisfactory, they can always go to the "local business" and either file a complaint or secure a refund.

A Rowan County, North Carolina, woman was approached by a man offering to caulk her gutters for $25. After checking the roof, he told her there was a considerable amount of rotting lumber on the roof, and she authorized him to do the repair. Subsequently, he and his crew presented her with a bill for $8,000. Although she balked at paying the bill, she felt threatened and finally gave the man a check for $2,500. Finally realizing that she had been the victim of fraud, the homeowner called her bank and tried to stop payment on the check. Too late! It had been cashed immediately.[10]

Apparently, this scam was similar to those perpetrated by an organization known as the Rocky Mount House-Mazza. Offering to clean gutters for a relatively small amount of money was the initial step this organization used to secure permission for a series of fictitious or unnecessary repairs. For example, a 92-year-old blind Raleigh, North Carolina, man was taken for $167,000 by the group from 1994 to 1996. A construction expert who had been hired by the state reported that the repair work that was necessary on the man's house could have been done for less than $2,000. According to the North Carolina Division of Aging, over 500 criminal convictions have been obtained against members of the House-Mazza organization, but its techniques are still in use.[11]

Spring and summer months are the most lucrative time for home repair con artists, and it seems amazing that people can be so vulnerable. One fleece artist warned an elderly woman in Chicago that her home had "cancer of the bricks." She depleted her bank account trying to keep the cancer from consuming her house. Another 75-year-old woman was persuaded to pay to have her sewer line dug up as the repairman said that he smelled radon gas in the basement.[12] She thought he was talking about fumes from her propane gas furnace and was afraid her home was going to explode.

Nicholas Visceglia, an 83-year-old retiree in Whitestone, New York, was surprised to see four men busily unloading ladders and canisters in his driveway. When he questioned the men, one asked him the location of his fuse box while another began roaming about the house examining the walls. Visceglia was told that he had a terrible water leak, that there was water dripping down his walls, that his fuse box was wet, and that the house was going to blow up if he didn't let them fix the problem. Fortunately for Visceglia, neighbors suspected something was wrong and called the police. Dan Parks, 70, his sons ages 50 and 45, and his 26-year-old grandson were arrested for attempted grand larceny. Apparently, the Parks family had focused on Visceglia because almost exactly a year before, he had been the victim of fraud for the amount of $6800 by men peddling a similar roof repair. "Well, I was almost nicked again, but that's it," Visceglia said in an interview to a *New York Times* reporter. "I've put a sign by the door saying 'no repairs.' I'll make my son do it from now on."[13]

The examples of successful scams on homeowners illustrate the many variations and appear to be endless. Hundreds, possibly thousands, of Californians have been cheated by home improvement scams, according to a report from the Consumers Union's West Coast Office. Most of the victims were elderly women, and many were of African-American or Latino heritage. Almost all had only small private pensions or minimum social security benefits. Because these individuals did not have available funds, the con artists conveniently offered to arrange financing. Apparently, most homeowners did not understand that their houses would be the collateral for these loans.[14]

Among the numerous cases reported was that of Josephine B., a 75-year-old widow. In 1991 she was approached at her Oakland home by a salesman for a painting contractor and was told that if she could not pay cash, a loan would be arranged. Shortly thereafter, Josephine was visited at her home by a loan agent from a finance company. Since she had limited reading ability, she did not read the extensive wording of the loan contract. She claimed that the loan agent only asked if she would be able to pay $140 per month on the loan. At no time did the loan agent inform her that, "in addition to the monthly payments, she would be responsible for a balloon payment of $11,200, which would be due in 7 years."[15] In the event that she could not fulfill the terms of the finance company's contract (which was then sold to another finance company), she faced foreclosure on her home.

San Franciscan Eva D. *did* lose her home. The 65-year-old widow was lured into a loan with a lender and contractor in order to repair damage done to her house during the Loma Prieta earthquake. Suffering from glaucoma, she could not read the loan document and was persuaded to sign a blank piece of paper. With an income of less than $1,200 per month, the lender arranged a loan of $150,000 and charged over 15 points ($23,000) in origination fees. Payments on Eva's loan were just under $2,000 a month. Repairs promised by the contractor—unlicenced as she discovered later— were never completed. Unable to make the payments, Eva's home was sold at trustee's sale, and she was evicted and carried out of the house in a wheel chair.[16] In situations like this, the victim must attempt to locate some type of affordable housing. Many times this is impossible to do, and the individual becomes an unwelcome guest in a relative's home.

Another elderly Californian didn't lose her home, but she discovered that her plumbing problem could generate horrendous charges. Discovering that her toilet was not functioning properly, she contacted a San Joaquin County plumbing contractor with the clever name Drain Patrol. The problem with the toilet was solved, but the 83-year-old woman received a bill for more than $10,000 for this necessary service.[17] In this instance, the district attorney filed a suit against the organization, contending that Drain Patrol committed both grand theft and elder abuse for taking advantage of this senior citizen.

Often unscrupulous contractors will quote an extremely low price for a repair or for remodeling and then demand a higher cost due to "unforeseen" expenses upon completion of the job, a tactic known as *buying in*.[18] The homeowners assume the bid is a firm price and that there will be no additional cost for the project. However, should the costs rise, as they inevitably do, homeowners are expected to cover the increase in the quoted price. If the additional cost is questioned, the explanation given by the contractor, and usually accepted by the homeowners, is that extra materials were needed. It is emphasized that the originally quoted price was merely an estimate—just a bid—not a final price. Most individuals have little recourse except to pay the higher cost, as is shown by one elderly couple who needed to remodel and enlarge a bathroom to accommodate a wheelchair. Originally, they were told by the contractor that they could purchase the new shower stall, vanity, toilet, doors, and so forth themselves from local discount stores and save considerable expense by doing so.

> We were able to get the vanity and medicine cabinet at the discount price, but when it came to the toilet we were told that the ones we had been looking at didn't meet some building requirement. We were also told that the shower stall we had chosen—one of those already premade and with a seat at one end—was not adequate for our needs. So, the contractor bought the toilet for us and then installed a tub and shower which had to be tiled. The tile was quite expensive, and I doubt that we ever use the tub as we both have trouble getting up or down.
>
> When the final bill came, we were horrified. It was nearly $1700 over what we had been quoted. We just didn't have that kind of extra money and complained, but it did us no good. The contractor merely explained that the toilet and shower he had installed was of better quality and higher in price than what we had originally con-

tracted for. We had to pay the bill or, possibly, have our credit ruined.

Another tactic often used by fraudulent contractors is known as *pyramiding profits*. The contractors either purchase materials or labor from subcontractors who also purchase other components from other subcontractors, with each charging cost plus profits.[19] Technically, this practice is legal, but each time it is used, the cost to homeowners rises. In a scam situation, usually there are no subcontractors, or if there are, these individuals are co-conspirators. Homeowners unaware of this practice and sometimes caught with only a partially completed project may feel they have no recourse except to file a civil suit. If they choose not to do this, their only option may be to pay the price increase. Probably most individuals are not even aware of the pyramiding profits concept.

In addition, even if the original contractor legitimately hired subcontractors, many times he does not pay them for their labor or materials. The homeowners have already paid the entire cost of the project to the contractor, who has kept the money. The subcontractors then have no choice except to bill the homeowners, who usually refuse to pay. At this point the subcontractors have the option to file a lien against the property for their services. Almost always the homeowners will pay up as they do not wish to have their property encumbered with a lien.

Even paying for a completed project can involve some hazard. Although most contractors who are perpetrating a scam hope homeowners will have ready cash to hand to them, they usually are willing to accept a check. Elderly individuals who have problems with eyesight or suffer from arthritis often have difficulty filling in the required amount. Some may neglect to indicate the name of the contractors on the check, assuming they will fill in their name or the company name. Some simply make the check payable to "cash." Once the check is cashed (and this is done quickly), the homeowners or the police, if the incident is reported, have no way to track down who actually took the money. Also, the con artists may now have additional information about their victims, such as phone numbers, social security numbers, and checking account numbers that are printed on most checks.

In addition, homeowners frequently are careless about giving contractors their credit cards to use when purchasing items for home repair. Instead of making the effort themselves to go to their local retail outlets that deal in materials for sprucing up one's home, individuals call the store and indicate that a particular contractor can charge whatever is needed. Dishonest contractors then purchase numerous items not necessary for the job, sell the excess material for a profit, or use it to complete some other job. The homeowners usually are unaware that excess material has been purchased until they receive their credit card statements. If the statements do not itemize the purchases, they may never realize they have been defrauded. In addition, many people simply do not take the time to check on charges listed on the statements, assuming that no mistakes have occurred.

Those individuals dealing with home improvement contractors should pay heed to the following warnings issued by the Houston, Texas, police department:

- Beware of home improvement salespersons who come to your door uninvited.
- Carefully evaluate what you want done before selecting a contractor.
- Get recommendations and check them out.
- Make comparisons. Most people comparison shop for many needed items.
- Get three estimates, and remember, the lowest may not be the best.
- If you decide to hire the contractor, check the individual's driver's license, jotting down the name, address, and date of birth.
- Above all, don't be rushed into quickly signing a contract
- Never, never pay in advance for the promised work
- Above all, never open the door to a caller unless you know the individual. Otherwise, *don't let them in your home*!

Once con artists have gained access to a mark's home, they are in control of the situation. Door-to-door salespeople prey on the elderly by getting into their houses and encouraging them to purchase all kinds of products. For example, hearing aids have been sold door-to-door for years, and some of the offers are scams. The elderly, hoping to regain their lost hearing, become willing victims as the salespeople promise them a new, happier life without being hearing impaired.

Hearing tests using simple earphones are often administered in the person's home with noise from traffic, ringing telephones, and air conditioners impeding the victim's ability to hear and making the tests invalid. One woman reported that the salesman told her he was a factory representative and that she was lucky, as he just happened to be in the area that day. Then he explained that she needed two hearing aids "right away and had to place the order now because he . . . wouldn't be back for 3 months. The cost of each aid was $2,000, but he could get me two for $3,500 and a 20 percent discount on top of that."[20] The catch was that the woman had to purchase the aids immediately to get the discount, and no mention was made of when she might receive the merchandise. Fortunately, that woman declined to get taken in, not because she thought the offer was a scam, but simply because she had no cash available for a down payment.

In addition to door-to-door salespeople offering free hearing examinations, these are advertised on television and in newspapers. After his daughter had seen such an advertisement, West Virginian Miles Kidd made an appointment for a free examination. The "hearing specialist" explained that Mr. Kidd would eventually lose all ability to hear unless he purchased two aids. However, Mr. Kidd was not taken in by the high-pressure sales pitch and only bought one aid at a cost of $975. What he discovered was that the aid dulled rather than enhanced sounds. Although he complained, he received no satisfaction from the hearing aid dealer. Eventually, Mr. Kidd stumbled across an article that indicated that the attorney general of his state was conducting an investigation of the dealership where he had made his purchase, and he was able to obtain a refund of $850 from the manufacturer of the unsatisfactory item.[21] Mr. Kidd was able to obtain a favorable solution to his problem, but many times the unfortunate victims cannot get a refund, or the perpetrators of the scam relocate before the victims realize they have been duped.

Although vacuum cleaner scams are not as numerous as once was the case, clever con artists still ply their trade in this area, particularly in smaller towns or rural areas. They, too, gain access to the victim's home in order to demonstrate the efficiency of their product. (It is interesting to note that an offer to clean a carpet "free of charge" or with "no strings attached" quickly gains admittance to some people's homes.) Often high pressure to buy is applied by the salespeople, and in the case of the elderly, the product they get may be too expensive for their budget or too heavy for them to use.

Free gifts are sometimes offered to the purchasers of vacuum cleaners. A free radio was the come on for one such purchase. In this case an elderly Hispanic woman living in New Mexico desired the free gift and agreed to buy the product just from listening to the sales pitch at her door. When the con artist brought the radio and the vacuum into her house, he discovered that she had no carpets or rugs of any kind. Her tiny home had only dirt floors. (This did not deter the man from selling the vacuum, however.)

The fake inspector is another scam that can net con artists a great deal of money. This individual will claim to be conducting a routine inspection of a fuse box, water meter, or heating unit.[22] Each October, particularly, homeowners will be approached by an "inspector" who needs to make a safety check on their furnaces. Once inside, the con artist makes a quick check, tells the tenants that certain parts have to be replaced, and just happens to have the necessary parts available. Similar to this is the furnace inspector who reports to the homeowners that their present heating element needs to be completely replaced. Shortly after this individual leaves the home, a furnace salesman just happens to be in the neighborhood and can provide them with exactly what they need. The homeowners, worried about a possible fire hazard or carbon monoxide poisoning, are quick to agree and pay an expensive price for cheap parts or a completely new product. Elderly individuals are especially prey to these kinds of scams as they are retired and are usually at home during daytime hours when con artists are prowling the area. Also, many are physically unable to check or repair heating elements and welcome the con artist into their houses.

Sometimes, if door-to-door salespeople feel they cannot make a sale, intimidation is applied. Sitting at a kitchen table or in the living room of the victims' homes, the salespeople often raise their voices, move closer and closer to victims, and nearly pen them into a corner. The elderly man or woman, feeling somewhat threatened by this, is usually convinced to make a purchase. As one interviewee explained, she felt coerced into purchasing a hearing aid.

> I just didn't know what to do. This man came to my door and just edged his way into the front room. He seemed pleasant and explained that he had gotten my name from a friend. He knew I couldn't hear too well and said he had a hearing aid that would correct my problem.
>
> I didn't want to buy the product and told him I didn't have but a few dollars in the house and was on social security. I couldn't afford a $1500 hearing aid. He said that Medicare would pay part of the bill, and he kept sitting there and talking louder and louder. He sort of scared me, and I couldn't seem to get rid of him. Finally, I said I would buy the thing and gave him the $69 I had in my purse as a down payment. It was all the money I had in the house. He left then, but I've never received the hearing aid, and I've never heard from him again. Thank heavens! I don't want to see him again.

Con artists are also quick to take advantage of new ways to fleece the unwary. Over the past couple of years, with interest rates dropping, unscrupulous individuals have been using the mail and telephones to offer homeowners the chance to refinance mortgages (Chapter 3). In addition, they have also used the door-to-door approach. These home equity scams are appealing to the elderly on a fixed income as they offer ready cash. Although many of these home equity refinancing offers are legitimate and carefully outline all pertinent terms and charges, some do not. For example, many lenders target those with low incomes or credit problems and take advantage of them by using deceptive practices. The Federal Trade Commission advises that some of these practices violate federal and state laws dealing with disclosures about loan terms and debt collection.[23]

Another scam, of which most people are unaware, is the "IRS agents" who come to the homeowner and indicate that they can get the individuals a *big* refund—for a fee, of course. The Internal Revenue Service warns that these con artists often want to "borrow" the homeowner's social security number or present a phony

W-2 form that appears to offer the refund.[24] The "agents" may offer to split the refund, asking for their share up front, explaining that the mark will be reimbursed when the full refund is received.

Even having a beautiful yard can be an invitation to become a scam victim. Retired people often have the time to spend in manicuring their lawns, growing hybrid roses, and generally making a showplace of their homes. Spotting homes such as this, the grifter who practices the Oak Tree Scam will soon be knocking at the homeowner's door. Explaining that he just happens to be in the neighborhood and noticing the lovely yard, he wonders if the homeowner would be interested in purchasing some small oak trees. If the mark is hesitant, the con artist may explain that he will sell the trees at a price well below that of the local garden stores.[25] Sometimes, as a further incentive, the con artist will offer to plant the trees purchased at no extra cost.

The mark agrees, and on the day of the planting, the con arrives with a truck, some shovels, and the bargain oak trees. When the planting is finished, the purchase price is collected and the con moves on to the next victim. Several days later, all of the newly planted oaks become wilted and die. When the mark examines the trees (or possibly calls someone from a local nursery), it is discovered that the trees are not diseased or damaged. The "trees" are merely oak branches planted in dirt and wrapped in burlap to disguise the lack of a root system. The con is gone and the mark is usually out several hundred dollars for oak branches.

Sometimes cons traveling in pairs will see an elderly man or woman busily raking leaves or pruning shrubs. One of the con artists will engage the victim in conversation, commenting on how hard the work is or how nice the yard looks, while the other slips into the house to look for valuables. Occasionally, the con poses as a policeman, real estate agent, or public official in order to gain a victim's attention and confidence.

Cons working in pairs also may use the old stalled car routine. One of the pair asks for permission to use the phone to call a tow truck. The victim thinks this is a reasonable request and permits them access to the home. Most times these individuals tend to be well dressed, very polite, and thankful for the victim's help. In this way they gain the trust of people who are neighborly and willing to help someone in trouble. As one man explained to the police:

Both the man and the woman wore suits. I thought they were business people. You know, maybe real estate agents out to show property. Their car was not working, so I found my telephone book and the man called a garage. The woman said she was thirsty, so I told her to get a glass of water from the kitchen. They thanked me for being kind enough to let them use my phone.

Then they walked back out in the yard with me and stayed and chatted for a few minutes. The woman asked me the name of some of my flowers, and I gave her a yellow rosebud off one of my bushes. It was several hours later before I found that my watch and billfold were missing from the chest in my bedroom.

There may be other things gone. . . . I simply don't know. You can't be a good neighbor these days.

Even though the mark may go inside the house with the two cons, as this man did, one distracts the mark while the other steals what is readily available or cases the home for a future burglary. This distraction burglary is often called burglary artifice, deception theft, or imposter burglary.[26]

Frank, an air-conditioning repairman, was an excellent example of distraction burglary. During customer service calls he gleaned information about the family's habits, many times learning when no one would be home. Frank was very thorough in the service he provided, taking a long time to check out equipment, tinkering with the air conditioner's mechanism, and examining the air ducts throughout the house. He also inspected the outside condenser and found the best route for a quick entrance and a fast getaway.[27] (In fact, many of those conned by Frank commented on how pleased they had been with the excellence of his inspections.)

One man in Florida practiced imposter burglary by posing as a subcontractor hired by the city housing association to inspect doorframes. He gained the confidence of elderly victims in two ways. First, he had identification and appeared to be an official of the town making required routine inspections, and second, he frequently took a child with him. He would explain that his wife worked and that the babysitter was ill, so he was "babysitter for the day." Usually the victims were completely distracted, chatting at length with the child or taking it into a kitchen area for candy or cookies. In one instance the con man stole a ring valued at $10,000 and another time was able to take over $40,000 worth of jewelry.[28]

OUTGOING MAIL

The media frequently highlights stories relating to mail fraud or mail theft (Chapter 3), but people don't expect culprits to steal the mail that they put in their front porch mailboxes for pickup by their carriers. However, it is not uncommon to drive through neighborhoods and see outgoing mail clamped to a mailbox with a clothespin. The elderly, particularly those who have difficulty getting to a street corner mailbox or post office, sometimes use this method. Most bills are still paid by check through the mail, and some senior citizens use pens that have erasable ink. The con artists steal the mail, erase and increase the checks' amounts, alter the name of the recipients, and substitute their names or the name of a fake company. (Even if erasable ink is not used, there are now products on the market that make it possible for ink on paper to be altered or eliminated without defacing the paper.) The victims do not usually realize there has been a mail theft until they receive notices indicating their accounts are past due. Upon investigating, they find that their bank accounts have been severely depleted and that some of their checks have been returned to creditors marked insufficient funds.

TELEPHONE SCHEMES

These are not the scams perpetrated by some telemarketers (Chapter 5); telephone schemes sometimes involve illegally changing service or gaining the use of another individual's phone. Most senior citizens are not in the workforce and tend to be available and willing to answer their home phones. Therefore, the elderly are receptive victims for those companies that wish to get individuals to change telephone service unwittingly, or cons who wish to make free long-distance calls.

In 2003, the Arizona attorney general's office warned the public about two common forms of telephone fraud: *slamming*, which changes long-distance carriers without consumers' consent, and *cramming*, which adds to consumers' service without their permission.[29] Seventy-two-year-old Elizabeth R. was "slammed" when she failed to read the fine print before signing a form presented to her by a representative of a telephone company.

> Just as I entered the gate at the Colorado State Fair, I saw a booth which had a sign saying I could make a free long-distance call anywhere in the world. When I questioned one of the people manning the booth, I was told that this was true. Jokingly, I asked if I could call Tibet and was assured that I could. It was free, so I said that I would like to telephone a good friend in Australia. No problem. All I had to do was sign a form that indicated I was making the call. This was so the phone company offering the free call would know that I was a legitimate caller, that the people who were running the booth had actually spoken with me, etc. So, without reading what was on the form—actually there wasn't very much printed on the form—I signed. A few weeks later I, and many other residents of Colorado, learned that by signing the form we had switched our telephone service. I complained, but it took a couple of months before I could get switched back to my original carrier.

If charges appear on monthly bills without the consumers' authorization, cramming has occurred. For instance, Maurice received a call at home one evening from a well-known telephone company's "technician." The technician stated that he was checking the phone lines and needed Maurice to hit the 9 key, the 0 key, the pound sign, and then hang up. Maurice followed these instructions, and the next month he found that he had numerous long-distance charges on his phone bill. Upon complaining to the phone company that he had not made the calls, Maurice was informed that the technician was not an employee, that the company had no knowledge of the incident, and that by pressing 90# he had given the perpetrator the right to utilize his phone for long-distance calls.

Another individual similarly contacted indicated that he "became suspicious and refused to follow the caller's instructions." After reaching his carrier, he was told that the telephone company was aware of the scam and that it had been originating from several local jails and prisons. Apparently, the inmates, with limited access or funds for calls, had discovered a way to make long-distance calls whenever they wished at unwary victims' expense.[30] This individual called local law enforcement and asked them to make the public aware of the scam.

Because there are now numerous phone companies available from which customers can select their service, it has become big business to solicit customers away from one company to another. One scam practiced a number of years ago was very clever. A representative would call and ask if an individual would like to switch to that particular phone company. The victim would say, "No, thank you. I don't want to switch to . . ." and give the name of the company calling. What the victims did not realize was that the company had cleverly manipulated the system so that by uttering that company's name, they had committed themselves to changing companies. It was not long, though, before the media publicized the scam, and it no longer got the desired results.

Sometimes optional services, such as voice mail, paging, or personal 800 numbers, may appear on a phone bill. This can happen because a contest entry form has been filled out, or individuals fail to respond to a negative sales pitch. Calling a 900 number may also cause problems. Another area code to resist dialing is 809. For example, a message may be left on the victims' answering machines, usually indicating a prize has been won, that there is an emergency regarding a family member, or that a company is threatening legal action on an overdue account. If the marks dial the 809 area code, they will discover that it is in the British Virgin Islands, and the cost for these calls can be $25 per minute. Obviously, the person answering the calls will attempt to keep the victims on the phone for a lengthy period in order to get the charges as high as possible.[31]

REPORTING THE SCAMS

In the past few years, across the country the media has been reporting scams and warning the public to beware. The National Crime Victimization Survey (which does not break down its statistics by age) states that elderly people may actually be less victimized because "they get smarter as they get older." However, it does not give any evidence to back up this generalization. Therefore, as the baby boomers rapidly move into the ranks of the elderly, unless they become more educated about scams, con artists will have a steady supply of senior citizens just "ripe for the picking."

With the high number of victims (of all ages) presently suffering from scams, one would think that law enforcement would be inundated with complaints or calls for help. However, this does not seem to be the case. In fact, the above survey found that "only a small percentage of incidents were reported to the authorities: just 15 percent overall."[32] It can be understood why some elderly are leery of letting anyone know they have been fleeced, as they feel this is an indication that they no longer have the mental capability to manage their lives. Children who are expecting to inherit from elders' estates may encourage or coerce elderly fraud victims to sign a power of attorney (Chapter 5). There is also the fear of possible retaliation by the perpetrators, if they should be arrested and have to stand trial. Unlike the women who came forth in the Arellano case (listed below), for most elderly individuals, the idea of having to appear in court and testify at a trial may be overwhelming. Then, too, family members, friends, and even police may humiliate them for "being so stupid."

Comments from law enforcement officials, which appear regularly in the media, indicate that when dealing with elderly homeowners who have been victimized, they invariably encounter the following problems:

- Victims did not ask for a driver's license or get the license number of the vehicle driven by the perpetrator.
- Victims did not ask for references or check with the Better Business Bureau.
- Victims did not telephone a local company to see if that company employed a particular individual or contractor.
- Victims did not report the scam until weeks or months after it had occurred, as they often were unaware of the problem until money was missing from an account or overdue bills arrived.
- Victims were unwilling to file official complaints, especially if the perpetrators might still be in the area.
- Victims expected the police to "do something" which would immediately get the missing funds returned. However, victims often had received a completed, or partially completed

service. Therefore, proving a scam can be difficult. Also, victims had often signed a contract; therefore, many times this is deemed a civil case as opposed to a criminal case.

Indicating to the victims that there is little law enforcement can do after the crime has been committed and the unidentified perpetrators have vanished is of little comfort to senior citizens who have lost irreplaceable sums of money or valuables. As one detective from Kansas City stated in a telephone interview:

> I sat in their den and listened to this elderly couple as they told me about how they had given two men money to repair their roof. It was not a huge sum, only $650. But to them it was a lot of money. They were living off social security checks and small, quarterly amounts of interest from some savings.
>
> The woman did most of the talking as the husband was nearly deaf and kept asking, "What? What did he say?" I could see how a con man could easily convince the couple to part with their money. The wife was not at all knowledgeable about roof repair, and the husband could not hear. It was a very sad situation, and they couldn't understand that it was much too late for me to do anything about their loss.

In another interview, a detective vented his frustration at the problems constantly faced with trying to pacify victims.

> This old woman literally cried on my shoulder. I sat in her small apartment and looked around at her home. She had nothing of value. The furniture was old and worn. She had met me at the door and needed a cane to walk. A clever guy had talked her into getting hardwood floors in her kitchen. She had paid him hundreds of dollars for a kitchen floor that was the size of a postage stamp. He did the flooring, but it was a laminated floor, not good-quality flooring. Shortly after it was down, it began to buckle and peel. Obviously, it had not been installed right.
>
> I questioned her about who the man was, what company did he work for, what guarantee was there on the work. She knew nothing, absolutely nothing, about the con artist. All I got from her was that his name was Fred, that he was fairly tall, and that she thought he had blonde to light brown hair. I had nothing to go on. I carefully explained this to her and sat there and just watched her cry as she said, "I don't have money left to pay the rent or my water and light

bill. How am I going to explain this to my kids?" There was just nothing I could do as I had nothing to go on. Even if I could have located Fred, if that was his real name, it would have been her word against his. There was nothing written down, no contract, nothing to say she had been taken. But both of us knew she had, and all I could do was just sit and listen.

Occasionally, there is a bright spot in these gloomy scenarios; some con artists are caught and prosecuted. Such was the case of parolee William Arellano who during 2003 was the perpetrator of a series of distraction burglaries against females ranging in age from 79 to 92. These victims *did* report the thefts. Arellano was apprehended, tried, and found guilty of burglary and two counts of attempted theft from an at-risk adult and one count of theft from an at-risk adult in connection with a series of home invasions. At his sentencing, Colorado Judge Scott Epstein indicated that Arellano was a career criminal and that his victims had a great deal of fear because of the case. He further admonished Arellano, eloquently stating, "These elderly ladies testified about the hell that they've gone through because of you. You stole not only their security, but their dignity. What you've taken is irreplaceable."[33]

Preventing these kinds of scams against the elderly is the aim of proactive law enforcement departments and government agencies. Today, most communities and states are taking steps to try to protect senior citizens. Recently, Colorado Attorney General Ken Salazar and the AARP Foundation designed a statewide clearinghouse to try to stop exploitation of the "most vulnerable" senior population. Known as the AARP ElderWatch, the mission of the project is "To ensure that no older person is left to suffer alone and in silence, at the hands of those who exploit them."[34] Among the areas targeted were home repair contractors and other home-related scams, and it was stressed that once individuals fall victim to one scam artist, others tend to flock to them, making them continually vulnerable.

Goals set for the project include connecting with law enforcement agencies and adult protective services, developing educational materials and presentations designed to prevent elderly people from becoming victims, and publishing consumer alerts about scams being perpetrated in various communities.[35] Frequently the media send out all sorts of safety tips to help protect homeowners from becoming victims. AARP's ElderWatch and the National Crime Prevention Council list the following:[36]

- Never use a full first name on mailboxes or in telephone directories.
- Never use the word "I" on an answering machine. Always use "we."
- For single women, have a male voice on the recording. This helps keep away those who prey on women living alone.
- Use a peephole or window to verify if a caller is legitimate. If still unsure, call the business the individual is representing. Do not simply open the door to strangers who ring the bell.
- Help protect the neighborhood by knowing the neighbors and contacting police if anyone appears to be suspicious.
- Always verify that the individual at the door is from a reputable company and is bonded.
- Ask for a photo ID.
- Ask the individual at the door to place a telephone call to you from his or her company office. Then call back to verify that call.
- Don't buy health products or treatments that promise a quick and dramatic cure.

It would seem that following these simple precautions should make the elderly less likely to become the victim of the con artists trolling their neighborhoods. Still, outwitting those who prey upon people in their homes is an almost impossible task. Now that some people have taken advantage of the National Do Not Call list, it is more difficult to reach millions of potential customers who were willing, maybe eager, to hear a voice on their phone. Therefore, many former telemarketing companies (Chapter 5) are returning to the old-fashioned door-to-door sales pitch. Michael Mullen knocks on doors in the Nashville area and rakes in nearly $650 a week selling discount coupon books. If the lady of the house answers his knock, Mullen says, "I'm sincere, ma'am, and if I weren't 100 percent sincere, I wouldn't be standing in front of you."[37] Certainly, Mullen may be sincere and his sales pitch and product a legitimate one; however, as more and more legitimate salespeople again utilize the door-to-door approach, con artists will also ply their trade.

Victimizing the public in their homes is the way these con artists have always made a living wage. It is a way of life for them, one they have practiced for years and one at which they have become very adept. It must also be remembered that in many cases senior citizens are their own worst enemy and aid in their victimization. For elderly persons, the con artist at their door is often a welcome relief from days or weeks of loneliness and endless boredom with only the companionship of the television set. They are eager to visit, share their problems, comment on world affairs, discuss their ailments—and part with their savings. Hopefully, more states will promote projects similar to AARP's ElderWatch and be able to prevent the elderly from sometimes being left penniless and stripped of their dignity by scams. Perhaps the elderly will help in this prevention by taking seriously the warnings about scams being perpetrated in their communities and becoming more wary of that "nice person" knocking on their front door.

Chapter Three

Through the Mail
(Snail Mail and E-mail)

* * *

They check the "obits" and then prey upon the bereaved.
—an Assistant District Attorney

* * *

P reying upon people mourning a recent death would appear to be one of the cruelest of all crimes, but it often has been the easiest. Most obituaries carried in newspapers no longer give the address of the deceased. It was soon discovered that doing so merely provided a chance for a clever thief to rob a home while family members were attending last rites for their loved one.

However, there are many other less-overt ways to get money falsely from the bereaved. In some situations, people known as funeral chasers visit or call the family of a recently deceased person and claim that the individual made a down payment on merchandise. Usually the family members are told that the merchandise was scheduled for delivery the next day, but there's a balance due that must be paid before delivery.[1] Most times the mourners do not question this and payment is made. Often, no merchandise ever appears, or, if a product is delivered, it is often of questionable quality.

Another scam that has proven successful is to mail a bill to the survivor for a purchase made by the deceased prior to his or her death. Many spouses, overcome with grief, do not always carefully check whether the merchandise was received or whether payment was already made. Older men and women, especially those whose spouses have taken care all of the family finances, are not usually aware of what has been paid or needs to be paid. They merely see the statement (sometimes marked past due) and remit the money.

Duplicate payment for "additional" funeral services also may not be discovered until long after the family member's death. This was what happened to 77-year-old Martha T., who still found it difficult to believe that con artists would take advantage of those suffering from the demise of a loved one.

> My husband of 55 years died, and I was heartbroken. I just couldn't seem to cope with everything that piled up on me after his death. I didn't realize until several months later when my daughter was going through the checkbook to help me balance it that I had received a bill for $5,000 from a company for additional funeral expenses for my husband's funeral. Without doing any further checking, I paid it as I needed to get all of the matters connected with his death taken care of. Then my daughter found out that I had already paid in full for the funeral. But I had sent the $5,000 to a post office box, and when we tried to trace the money, we found the box was no longer in existence. I know that I should have checked things out more carefully, but I was so upset over his death. I just didn't realize that someone would take advantage of me in my mourning. What heartless people!

Of course, financial exploitation of senior citizens regarding funerals does not always begin after death. Some have received in their mailboxes offers to purchase pre-need funeral packages. One woman in her late sixties (and still employed full-time) received a solicitation at her office, which is located in a large office building. On the envelope her office number was highlighted in yellow. Because most people had no idea of her exact location in the building, she felt that one of her coworkers probably had some connection with a funeral home and had provided this specific information to the company. She felt this was no coincidence and that she would receive additional solicitations to prepurchase funeral arrangements.

Many individuals do take on the chore of arranging their funerals early in order to save their loved ones the hassles involved in hurriedly doing so after their death. Although most funeral homes carefully adhere to presigned contracts for the burial or cremation, heirs may find that others fail to provide the expected services. Some providers mismanage or embezzle the money that had been placed in trust for future needs. Some may go out of business before the prepaid contract can be fulfilled, or if a new firm buys the business, it may be hesitant to honor all old contracts. Also, as AARP notes, some pre-need funeral providers "aggressively market products and services that consumers do not want and do not need, inflating prices and including vague terms and conditions in their contracts."[2] One 70-year-old woman encountered a hard sell when she arranged to prepay her cremation expenses.

> I was told that state law required that I have my ashes placed in a container so that my family could pick them up. The funeral director then showed me a number of urns which ranged in price from $160 to over $500. I asked if I couldn't have the family bring in a container as I knew I could go to Walmart or the nearest Hobby Lobby store and buy an urn or vase for about $19.95. Also, I knew that my ashes were scheduled to be scattered rather than kept for posterity, so my family didn't need to purchase an expensive urn. The director told me again that, by law, this wasn't allowed. The ashes had to be taken from the funeral home in one of their containers. Finally, I asked what the cheapest container would be and was told that the ashes could be put in a cardboard box which only cost $45. Forty-five dollars for a cardboard box! I told them that I could get a little white "take-out" container with a metal handle from a Chinese restaurant that could serve the purpose very well. Apparently, they didn't find this suggestion too amusing. In fact, the person talking with me looked like I had committed a crime for even suggesting such a thing. At any rate, I paid the $45 for a container to hold my ashes until they can be sprinkled somewhere a few days after I die. What a rip-off! I have the money to pay for such expensive and stupid funeral requirements, but what about those who don't have it—or their relatives for that matter?

Like this woman, many elderly make funeral arrangements early. When doing this, an individual should always be sure to read the fine print and find out if there will be any additional charges. For example, if the person wishes to be cremated, but the family would like a viewing of the deceased prior to the cremation, there is usually an extra charge of several hundred dollars for the rental of a coffin. Little details like this can add up to big money in total funeral cost.

If a traditional funeral is desired, today there are casket stores outside funeral homes that may help a family save money on this needed item. Of course, funeral homes are unhappy about the growing competition and wish to prevent families from taking advantage of this money-saving option. Therefore discount packages from funeral homes, which come through the mail or are advertised in local newspapers, promise savings of thousands of dollars. Some of these are sham discount packages and may end up costing the unwary buyer more because the funeral home will then raise its prices for services that may not be included in the special funeral package—collecting the body, chapel rental, limousine to the cemetery, memorial cards, and similar services. If the bereaved is elderly—often grief-stricken, bewildered, and with no one to help with arrangements—this individual probably will not ask for the home's general price list before making a decision about the funeral. Thus, those left behind may end up having to get a loan or make monthly payments to clear the funeral debt.

For individuals on mailing lists that target the elderly (such as lists available on the Internet, which are used by catalog companies selling products to the elderly, AARP, etc.), the mail scams described above are only a few of the numerous scams that fall into their mailboxes daily. The U.S. Postal Service delivers 180 billion pieces of mail each year. Among the legitimate products and services offered are many scams sent by "mailbox bandits."[3] Because e-mail has now taken over much of what would normally be received in snail mail, a large number of scams are now perpetrated over the Internet. It is not an easy task to weed out the fraudulent from the legitimate offers. Sham solicitations tend to be eye-catching, professional-looking, skillfully worded, and usually very convincing.

THE NIGERIAN SCAM

Over the past few years a major scam from overseas has popped up across the United States, tempting people of all ages to participate, including many senior citizens. This is the Nigerian

Letter Scam (also known as the Nigerian Advance Fee Scheme or the 4-1-9 scam), which arrives via both snail mail and, for many elderly who now are computer literate, through e-mail. This scam "has become so large in scope that it has been said to rank as Nigeria's third-largest industry."[4] Many Americans have received letters from individuals reportedly living in Nigeria and needing help in getting large sums of money transferred from that country to American banks. Most of them begin with a desperate plea such as "It is with heart full of hope that I write to seek your help," or "Only your kindness can help my desperate situation." Although referred to chiefly as the Nigerian scam, recently these pleas have also been coming from Liberia, the Ivory Coast, and South Africa, as the following example shows:

Attention My Dear,

VERY URGENT BUSINESS TRANSACTION

By way of introduction, my names are Mr. James C. Zulus. I am a citizen of South Africa . . . a Manager in a Trust Bank here. . . . I was privileged to have been the Account Manager of an expatriate customer . . . who is now deceased . . . without any beneficiary, or next of kin. . . . If nobody comes forward to ask for this money very soon, the Bank will legally appropriate/claim the whole money . . .

After the individual receiving the letter has been assured that the writer is only soliciting cooperation and collaboration for the two of them to appropriate the money in the dormant account, the scam begins in earnest. The mark is sucked in by being told that the account holds 57 million in U.S. dollars. The letter continues:

Essentially I need you to provide facility for the receipt of the money in bank accounts . . . outside South Africa. . . . I will first move to your nominated bank account the sum of $35,000,000.00 (Thirty-five million US dollars), before coming for the balance. This US $35m will be to our mutual benefits and you will be entitled to at least 25% of it, as your commission, on the completion of the transaction.

All of these letters promise big rewards that are difficult for almost anyone to reject. Many also suck in the religious or sympathetic person with salutations such as "Dearest in GOD," "Kindest of Person," or "with heart full of hope" and indicate that the person who helps will be "blessed by GOD" or "kept in GOD's eternal thoughts." The victim is further urged to be sure to respond because the writer knows of that person's "goodwill and trustworthiness." All of the letters ask for an immediate response, and many indicate that by sending the recipient's bank account information, this kind and generous American will not only be blessed but will "save my family and I from a hopeless future."

The usual amounts of money to be transferred are always in the millions of dollars, and commissions offered run from a low of 10 percent from an Ivory Coast solicitation to as high as 35 percent in some others. Who could resist such profitable transactions? The commission is enormous, and on a transaction that the scam artist assures the victim is "most civilized and noncriminal, meets internationally acceptable standards of practice and morals, and has no risk of failure." This scam has seduced all types of individuals— the rich, smart investor as well as the small businessman and the elderly pensioner.

The Nigerian scam has been around since 1987 and used to arrive chiefly through the postal service. Now, consumer reports to the Internet Fraud Watch (IFW) program and the National Consumers League (NCL) indicate that the Nigerian money offers are the fastest-growing fraud via e-mail. According to the NCL this type of fraud increased 900 percent within only one year, from 2000 to 2001. On an April 25, 2002, AT&T Worldnet daily poll, 12 percent of the nearly 27,000 respondents indicated that they had received unsolicited Nigerian letters.[5]

In 1997 the U.S. government estimated that the country's citizens were losing over 300 million dollars a year to the Nigerian scam. One man spent 5.2 million dollars and went as far as suing a bank in Nigeria in U.S. courts before he even knew he had been conned.[6] Some contributors have been lured to Nigeria and, in addition to losing a great deal of money, have been imprisoned (even killed) because the schemes violate section 419 of the Nigerian criminal code. Naturally, since the victim has conspired to remove funds from Nigeria, the government is not sympathetic to these individuals.[7] With warnings about this scam and stories of people who have become victims appearing frequently in the media, either people's greed overcomes caution, or they truly wish to be charitable.

Under a mandate to protect U.S. currency and financial institutions, since 1995 the U.S. Department of Commerce and the Secret Service have been working with Nigerian and other authorities to try to counteract this type of fraud. Sometimes this is difficult to do because there are variations on the scam, such as the Black Currency Scam. Brian Wizard of Oregon was taken in by a request from Nigerian cons to pay $8,000 to help them purchase special chemicals to "clean" a suitcase that supposedly was crammed with illicit U.S. $100 bills. He was told that each bill had a smudge on its face so that as it passed through U.S. Customs, it could not be detected. Wizard was convinced also that there was a great sum of money in a vault, of which he would receive $32 billion dollars.[8]

Although rare, occasionally victims receive more sinister scam notices. In Europe victims are sent "notifications of assassination" through what is termed a Threat Scam. Individuals purporting to be from an international security service send letters indicating that the recipient or a member of the family is going to be kidnapped and murdered. The solution to this threat, of course, is to pay huge sums of money to the security service for protection. People, fearful that the threat is a real one, pay up. Jim Caldwell, a supervisor in the Secret Service's financial crimes division explains, "They [the scams] may sound like old 1920s flim-flam, but they still work."[9]

SNAIL MAIL

Now that some people have placed their names on Do Not Call lists, those perpetrating scams via the telephone (Chapter 5) will once again have to resort to the postal service to seduce or confuse individuals. In December 2003, post cards reading "Special Customer Communication" appeared in mailboxes of those who had subscribed to various magazines. The message, written in extremely small print, thanked the addressee for being a valued customer. Then, if people didn't read further, they would find themselves paying for additional magazines, even if they hadn't renewed a subscription. Among the magazines mentioned were *Woodworking, Better Homes and Gardens, Sound & Vision,* and *Popular Photography & Imaging.* The customer was told the following:

The order you previously placed through your credit card provider to receive magazines will continue for the next term of issues using the credit card you previously provided for your selections and will be charged annually. . . . If you do not wish to continue, call 866 560 9273 by Jan 9 and no charge will appear. As long as you are satisfied, your selections will continue through our open-ended, customer friendly subscription method. . . .[10]

If customers read the entire card, they were told that a courtesy reminder would be mailed each year and that they could cancel at any time; however, many people would assume this was only another piece of junk mail and would end up tossing it in the trash. If they did not make the required telephone call, their credit card would be charged, and magazines would keep arriving. Of course, there is nothing illegal about sending out this communication, but one wonders why its message is so carefully hidden in such small print that is often missed by the senior citizen. The unwary may suddenly find an unexpected charge appear on their credit cards.

Another scheme that often arrives in the mailbox is lottery offers, and the opportunity to make an easy dollar has made victims putty in the hands of hustlers. Widower Richard Farley is an excellent example of someone who became a victim of several different lottery offerings that he had received in his mailbox—Canadian lotteries, Australian lotteries, and even British lotteries. His children were unaware that the 93-year-old California man was throwing away their inheritance until his son from Louisiana went for a visit. The 34 pieces of mail from such companies as *Reader's Digest*, Time Warner, and American Publishing House, along with a garage full of prizes, were clues that his father was spending his life's savings and his children's chances for any inheritance. Investigating further, the son read letters from such places as The Lottery Connection, which requested *another* $3,556 for lottery packages, and from Opportunities Unlimited, which offered a share of a $12,500 prize by merely adding the numbers 5+3+4+5+6 and writing the total on a line of the entry form.[11]

From Winner's, a letter to Farley introduced a Spanish lottery entitled Elgordo, that was supposedly the largest lottery in the world. Farley was told there was a one in six chance of winning the $1 billion jackpot by just sending $60,000 for the winning numbers. Project Rainbow from Vancouver promised 1400 chances to win for the excellent lottery value of only $899.00. An Australian lottery, the Millionaire Club, did send a check for $20 but encouraged Farley "to reinvest the check by purchasing more lottery numbers to 'upgrade' membership status."[12]

Perhaps the most original lottery scam was from a woman calling herself a "Metaphysical Super-Natural Adviser." In her letter she indicated that she had been awakened from a deep sleep by someone "who had passed over to the other side" poking her in the ribs. This spirit told her to contact Farley as he had been chosen to have a "magnificent Golden Miracle" coming into his life in the form of winning a lottery. To get this, all he had to do was send $19.95 for his miracle reading.[13]

IT'S FREE!

Free! That magic four-letter word makes most people throw away common sense, respond to ridiculous requests, and assume that they are going to get something for nothing. Brochures arrive daily in the nation's mailboxes, and particularly around holidays, spouting such slogans as "Buy one, get one free." What the average buyer may not realize is that the price of the one item has been increased to cover the cost of the "free" item. These "free offers" are mailed out by all sorts of merchandisers. Among the most prevalent are those involving book and music clubs, magazine subscriptions, sweepstakes, and merchandise advertised on television.

Received in the mail from book publishers or distributors is the enticing call. "HURRY—fill out your Booklovers' Survey today [and receive FREE gifts]. Your opinion is important to us," the addressee is told. However, this is not just a survey to discover what the public wishes to read; it entices the unwary into a book club where they can purchase (plus shipping and handling) five books for 99 cents. Sometimes the buyer actually may get free gifts—a wooden photo frame, a pen, a tiny jewelry box, a lighted key chain, an amazing coin purse, a letter opener, or similar items. Most of these are "gimmie gifts," merely inexpensive trinkets that the purchaser does not need and may not even want.

For those who do take advantage of the book club's offer, the catch usually is that they have agreed to purchase up to six more books within a particular period of time. If those who decided to join the book club have second thoughts, they are instructed to wrap the "introductory books" in a shipping carton and send the package back to the club. Sometimes the return postage is prepaid; sometimes it is not. The problem for many elderly is that they either can't or don't read the entire sales packet and end up getting additional books for which they are billed. Also, they may be physically unable to get to a post office to return the unwanted merchandise. Although this type of solicitation is not illegal, it often causes problems other than merely returning books. If individuals are unable or forget to pay the cost of additional books, their credit rating may suffer. In addition, their names have now appeared in a database, whereby other sales pitches of this type are routed to their homes.

Another clever way for salespeople to trap the unwary into purchasing an item is to send a postcard that asks the receivers to call a telephone number about a contest, prize, or sweepstakes entry. This type of offer appears to be common. A National Consumers League survey discovered that 92 percent of adults had received in the mail at one time or another a postcard or letter informing them that they had won "free prizes." Nearly 54 million people responded to the offers, but less than 20 percent received the promised prizes—unless, of course, they bought products or paid fees.[14] If the victims call to check on the status of the offer, they usually do get some bit of information about the prizes or the dates on which prizes will be awarded. However, most times, they will also get a sales pitch about a magazine subscription that is free. Usually the magazines are free only for a limited time, and the subscription then may require monthly payments for magazines that can be purchased for less at a local bookstore, newsstand, gas station, or other retail outlet.

The Christmas season 2003 saw "free notices" for all sorts of items flooding mailboxes. One was supposedly from an individual named Chris Moore, Awards Coordinator, and explained that Moore had been unable to reach the recipient about a free gift. "Please call 1-800-728-3902 within the next 5 days to find out how to receive your FREE George Foreman Grill," the notice urged. Upon calling the listed telephone number and inquiring about the free grill, an individual with a pleasant, helpful voice explained that a new storm window product was being tested in the caller's area. The caller was merely one of many selected to preview the product and was told that someone could be at her home within 5 days to provide a demonstration. When the 72-year-old female caller stated that she thought the postcard was merely a come-on to try and sell a product, the voice on the telephone became much less friendly, and the connection was immediately broken. Obviously, hundreds of thousands of these types of solicitations are in the mail daily; thousands of people respond, hoping or believing they will receive the free item listed. Even if they decide to "test the product" and let a salesperson into their home, or even if they do not succumb to pressure to do this, their name and phone number now may be on a list available to all comers—legal or fraudulent.

Even charities use the free gimmick and mail items that have not been requested by the postal patron. Giving to charity to help less-fortunate people is an admirable gesture, but individuals should begin to wonder about where and how their donations are being spent. In its Web site about charity fraud, the Department of Justice discusses the unscrupulous groups that prey upon the giving nature of citizens, misrepresenting its fundraising intentions or soliciting funds for phony causes (Chapter 5). However, it also alerts individuals that contributions may be going to a well-intentioned charity that may be spending its funds inefficiently or "primarily using its money on more fundraising appeals."[15] Several well-known, legally registered charitable organizations repeatedly mail packets of free holiday cards, calendars, note pads, or address labels, each time requesting another donation. For 69-year-old Jewel N., the repeated mailings became a problem.

> When I got the first set of address labels, I thought they were nice as they had my name and address correct and had varied designs for the holidays on them. So I responded with a check for $15 as I knew this was a legitimate charitable organization. Two weeks later another set of different labels arrived with another donation form. Again, although I waited about a month, I sent in money. Two weeks later, more address labels. I wrote on the donation form not to send another set of labels. I must have been writing to a computer, because I kept getting labels. When I stopped sending donations, I repeatedly got bills from this charity, but I refused to send additional money. After about a year, the duns for money finally stopped from that charity. But, I found out I must have been put on

a mailing list for other charities as I started getting labels from all kinds of places.

Although there definitely is no obligation to make a donation to any charity, like Jewel, people may feel pressured to keep sending checks if they receive a bill or more products. For seniors, additional donations may put a strain on their budgets. Also, they may wonder if their donations are merely being used for more fundraising appeals.

FINANCIAL FRAUD

Problems in the economy affect those of all ages; for elderly people on fixed incomes, a downturn can be particularly disastrous. Negative changes in the economy are alarming to those seniors who may have little in investments or savings accounts. Therefore, they look for all sorts of areas in which they can recoup losses or save what resources they still have. Any economic change can furnish a wealth of opportunities for the clever con artist; among these are various types of seminars designed to make or protect money. In a consumer fraud alert, the North Carolina Division of Aging warns seniors to be extremely skeptical about investment seminars marketed through newspaper, radio, or cable television infomercials. Those getting rich from the seminars are the people running them, "making money from admission fees and the sale of books and audiotapes."[16]

One recent scam, which cropped up in Colorado and targeted elderly, retired individuals, used the always-effective word *free* and provided seminars on estate planning. Through direct-mail flyers, seniors were invited to attend free seminars where they were told by Colorado Springs attorney Robert Mason and his associates, Harry Hochstetler and Claude Ray Page, about their "family asset protection" plans. Supposedly the plans would permit purchasers to shield their assets and still qualify for Medicaid to pay any nursing home costs. Charges for an estate plan ranged from $2,000 to $3,000, and it was estimated that more than 700 seniors had purchased plans. However, as these consumers incurred nursing home costs, they quickly learned that they were not qualified for Medicaid and had to pay the nursing home costs themselves.[17]

Fortunately for some elderly, in one community local law enforcement "encouraged" those setting up one of the seminars to move on. Still, in some towns unwary attendees had been asked to and had filled out a questionnaire listing all of their assets—home, insurance, stocks and bonds, savings and checking account, automobiles, and other possessions.

Edith Allison (who died recently at age 91) was one victim who spent $1850 for papers from Mason, hoping to preserve $120,000 in savings that would go to help her granddaughter with college. The asset protection plan was of no help. "She was told she could protect her assets," said her son Donald Allison in an interview with an *Associated Press* reporter. "It sounded too good to be true. Now we know [that it was]."[18]

Through inquiries and complaints from consumers, police departments, and several district attorney's offices, Colorado's Attorney General Ken Salazar filed a consumer fraud case against those selling the family asset protection plans. Commenting on the consumer fraud, Salazar stated, "Seniors have a great deal of anxiety and uncertainty about providing for family or for themselves late in life. These defendants took advantage of those fears and created a completely false hope that these victims could use the defendants' estate plan to shield their assets and qualify them for Medicaid payment of nursing home care expenses."[19]

In this case the attorney general's office sought restitution to injured consumers and in early 2004 won a $1.7 million judgment against the accused. The other two defendants had agreed earlier to pay $1 million in damages plus another $400,000, bringing the total amount in the case to $3.1 million. However, many seniors who participated in this scheme either died while the case was in court or ended up losing any savings after waiting too long to buy nursing home insurance at an affordable rate. Assistant Attorney General Jay Simonson indicated that the elderly had done all the right things by seeking professional help to protect their investments. He summed up the problem by stating, "They simply made the mistake of relying on a deceptive lawyer."[20]

For other seniors facing a weak economy, a bear market that has cut into retirement portfolios, and low interest rates that have reduced their fixed incomes, home equity can provide a source of supplemental income or a way to consolidate debts. Seminars on refinancing a home or offers through the mail for homeowners to obtain first or second mortgages on their home equity seem to arrive weekly. Many begin, "Dear Michael and Susan," as though the writer knows the couple personally. The letter indicates either the estimated value of the home or, possibly, the amount of any mortgage presently on the property. (This figure can be easily obtained on the Internet.) Usually an enticing rate of interest is listed, along with the items "Less Than Perfect Credit—OK" and "No Out of Pocket Costs." Although there is nothing illegal about this type of proposal, when making application for the loan many people fail to understand that they may have to pay a much higher rate of interest than quoted if their credit rating is bad. Also, they may not have to give the lender any cash from their pocket, but there are costs involved in setting up any loan. These costs will be included in the overall loan, and the borrowers will pay them off, with interest, in monthly payments. In addition, many of these letters include a "Quick-app" that asks for a great deal of personal information, including social security numbers, gross monthly income, additional income, reason for the loan, and signed permission for the lender to obtain credit information. Once this information is provided, even if the loan is never processed, homeowners' personal information may now be made available for others to offer services or products.

Taking out home-equity loans without careful consideration could put the family home at risk because, unlike most other forms of debt, failing to make home-equity loan payments may place a home in foreclosure. Most senior citizens have a great deal of equity in their homes, and, if this is the way they decide to go, they should be sure to shop carefully for a reputable lender. "Predatory lenders target older people whom they suspect don't understand equity loans and tend to charge extraordinarily high rates and fees," writes David Yeske, president of the Financial Planning Association. "Some even have bankrupted homeowners."[21]

The American Association of Retired Persons filed a suit in 1998 (which resulted in a $60 million settlement) against California-based First Alliance Mortgage Company after receiving numerous complaints from older consumers about the company's practices. Although most mortgage lenders charge 2 percent of the total loan for origination fees, First Alliance was charging between

10 and 25 percent. According to AARP Executive Director Bill Novelli, "Older people are major targets of predatory lenders . . . because nearly 80 percent of people over 50 own their own homes. . . . We've heard many of them say, 'They didn't tell me I could lose my home.'"[22]

Those seeking home equity loans are warned by various consumer protection services to beware if a potential lender offers a loan with small monthly payments that may "balloon" into a large final payment, which may pose a big problem for those with low monthly incomes and limited savings. Also if the lender pushes to have a signature on the application immediately or requests a fee up front, don't be taken in by these tactics. This is the typical advance fee loan, and, often, the lender may get the money and is never seen again.

Today, attractive brochures arrive in the mail touting the advantages of downsizing from a larger home as individuals reach their retirement years. Many elderly people are looking at manufactured homes because these houses are very spacious, attractive, and require little maintenance. Again, without reading the loan application or contract thoroughly, seniors can get into financial trouble. One 84-year-old gentleman explained what had happened to him when he decided to take advantage of one of these mail offers.

I wanted to move back to my home state, so I sold my house and spent most of the proceeds to get back home. I got a mail flyer, went to a modular home place, and they sold me a great home. I was so excited. I told them that I had only a very small down payment, and my only income was my social security check. They said that was no problem, and I signed the papers. I didn't read them as I have a hard time reading because my eyes aren't very good.

Three months later I lost the home and had to move in with my son in the state I left. To get me financing for the modular, the sellers had listed my income as $3,000 a month. The monthly house payment was twice what my social security was. I think they did this because they knew I could not have gotten a loan otherwise. It was my problem as I had signed the papers without reading them. Actually, when I signed I was indicating that all of the figures on the application were accurate. I should have read them, but I trusted the modular people. My credit wasn't too good when I applied for the loan, and I'll bet it's worse now, but they told me that bad credit was no problem and went ahead and sold me the house. Maybe that should have been a warning to me.

If told that poor credit is no problem, or that a credit repair company can correct any problem, beware. This may be a rip-off. Take the case of Charlene Blanchard, whose credit rating was so bad she couldn't even get a loan for an automobile. She turned to a credit repair firm that promised to fix her credit in 3 months for a fee of $70. "Nothing came off my credit report—not one lousy thing. I got gypped out of my money," stated Blanchard, a nursing home clerk in Baltimore.[23]

Although it is time-consuming, people can improve their credit reports by checking to see if information listed is accurate and by challenging inaccurate information. However, credit repair firms cannot simply erase bad credit as they often advertise. Also, by law they must provide written contracts in advance and cannot charge until they have provided the promised services. Even so, these repair firms offer little to those with bad credit ratings. People should be aware, as C. Steven Baker, director of the Federal Trade Commission's Midwest regional office in Chicago, says, "There's no magic bullet to fix a bad credit report."

CREDIT CARD OFFERS

With the slump in the stock market, many seniors on a fixed income began to look at options to stretch their budgets because they see monthly income dwindling. One of the tempting offers many credit card companies send in the mail is an option to transfer any balances on high-interest cards to "zero percent interest" for varying periods of time. While it must be emphasized that *these offers are legal,* sound good, and sometimes can be very beneficial to those short of cash, there can be some pitfalls of which many people are unaware. This low interest rate usually is not the same as a bank loan agreement where interest rates and other terms are spelled out. The interest rate can change—always to a higher rate—for a number of reasons depending on the credit card company. On one agreement, if a customer does not make at least two required monthly purchases, the credit card company is permitted to raise the low interest rate; if payment is late twice on another card, the rate could go from the low zero percent to as high as 19.99 percent and steep late fees may apply; if one credit card company feels consumers are carrying too much debt compared with their resources, terms of payment and interest rates may change. "That's why it's such a land mine for consumers," said Linda Sherry, a spokeswoman for the consumer-advocacy group Consumer Action. "You have to tread very carefully or it could blow up in your face."[24] Obviously, credit card companies are not in business merely to be kind to consumers. They want these individuals to make a mistake in following the terms of the contract so the companies can make money. Consumers need to be aware of what they are taking on with credit card purchases or balance transfers.

Again, although *not legally a scam*, letters enticing people to cash unsolicited checks mailed out by almost all credit card companies can cause severe problems for the elderly. Often standard pitches such as, "We think you'll agree—*having more cash makes the holidays merrier*," are guaranteed lures for those elderly on a fixed income who wish to be able to provide presents to family members but do not have the funds to do so. Usually the pitch urges the recipient to "use the enclosed checks and your low 0% Annual Percentage Rate . . . through your statement closing date . . . to give yourself and your friends a truly wonderful holiday party." In parenthesis or at the bottom of the letter are those other words, "Transaction fees apply." The addressees, however, see only the attached blank checks imprinted with their names and the call to make this Christmas season the "happiest of holidays for those who mean so much to you." Who could resist such a chance? Many don't, and write checks for amounts that they cannot repay within the designated billing cycle. Thus they end up forking over monthly payments at much higher interest rates. The solution to this problem is *tear up those checks!*

TAX SCAMS

The Internal Revenue Service (IRS) has indicated that there is a "dirty dozen" of common scams that come in the mail and involve paying taxes. Among these are:

- Phony "tax payment checks" called sight drafts, which con artists sell to pay a tax liability, mortgage, or other debts. The checks are worthless and have no financial value.

- Social Security tax schemes that offer refunds of *all* social security taxes paid over a lifetime. The scam gets the victim to pay a "paperwork fee" of $100.

- Promises of a big refund, which asks victims to lend their social security numbers or a W-2 form, and they will get a portion of an unusually large return.

- Share or borrow dependents, whereby those with only one or a few children may borrow or share the dependents from larger families in order to get the maximum deductions. The preparer and the client "selling" the extra dependents split a fee paid by the victims needing the extra deductions.

- Slavery reparations, in which con artists have promised thousands of black Americans (for a fee) that they can get tax credits or refunds related to slavery reparations.

- IRS impersonators making house calls to collect income taxes and save the payee the trouble of a trip to the post office.[25]

As the IRS points out, many of the con artists use personal information gained from these frauds for identity theft. They advise that there is no secret or clever way to get out of paying taxes and that anyone suspecting tax fraud should call the IRS.

DON'T OPEN THAT PACKAGE!

Another clever scam is shipping merchandise that was not ordered. For example, let's assume that Mary Jane ordered a cookbook that she has seen advertised on television. A few weeks after the ordered book arrives, another package from the same company finds its way into her mailbox. If Mary Jane does not open the package, it can be marked "refused," and the post office will return it to the sender at no charge to Mary Jane. However, if she *opens* the parcel and discovers it is not a product she ordered, then she will have to pay the return postage. Although not considered one of the bigger scams, shipping unwanted merchandise can be very annoying and, sometimes, costly.

To defend oneself against mailbox fraud, the individual must be ever-vigilant as those postcards and letters promising unlimited wealth are hard to reject. However, there are some things one can do.[26]

- Don't pay for a *free* gift. If it's free, you shouldn't have to send any form of reimbursement, not even shipping and handling charges.

- If a solicitation appears to be a government document, toss it in the trash or shred it. The government doesn't solicit funds for any project.

- If you receive an unsolicited check in the mail (and dozens of these tend to arrive near holidays), be sure to read the front *and* back. If a person cashes one of these checks, he or she may be agreeing to be billed for something not wanted.

- Be sure to document any transactions and keep the envelopes because these are proof that the mail was used for fraudulent solicitations.

- If you do decide to respond to the solicitation, check with the attorney general or Better Business Bureau. However, this may not be foolproof as there may be no complaints against an organization, especially if it is new in the area or if it has had a name change or new ownership.

One other way to help gain protection from mail fraud is to "opt out." Financial institutions may share customers' information with other companies. However, each year these institutions should send a privacy notice with instructions for opting out.[27] If this choice is made, it should reduce unsolicited offers. (On the other hand, it could mean that the customers may not receive desirable offers in their mailboxes.)

For years the United States Postal Service has made an effort to halt mail fraud. Postal inspectors have led fraud prevention projects and participated with various groups, including consumer protection agencies, to help citizens become aware of mail scams before they could become victims. In April 2000, the Deceptive Mail Prevention and Enforcement Act was passed and became law. It protects consumers, particularly seniors, against deceptive mailings and sweepstakes practices. (Sweepstakes and illegal contest schemes are among the most common examples of mail fraud against consumers.) Because of this law, there are approximately 300 postal inspectors whose job it is to conduct mail fraud investigations, including fraud against senior citizens. "In 2002 postal inspectors arrested 1,634 mail fraud offenders, and 1,453 were convicted. As a result . . . there was more than $2 billion in court-ordered and voluntary restitution."[28]

In another attempt to protect its customers, the U.S. Postal Inspection Service sent to each of the nations' 120 million households a postcard that warned them about direct-mail fraud.[29] This card emphasized a host of gimmicks, including sweepstakes and prize promotions, overseas lotteries, letters from foreign nationals asking to transfer funds, and similar scams that bombard American mailboxes each year. Hopefully, this postcard helped some elderly targets avoid mailbox fraud.

Chapter Four

Identity Theft

* * *

But he that filches from me my good name
Robs me of that which not enriches him,
And makes me poor indeed.
—Othello, act iii, scene 3

* * *

The fake Michigan driver's license bore the name of victim Jane S. but another woman's photo. With it, the impersonator walked into an American Express office, claimed she'd lost her credit card, and asked for a replacement. The helpful American Express representative handed one over, and the shopping spree began. The binge included stops at two jewelry stores, an appliance store, and Saks Fifth Avenue. "They even had the nerve to buy Versace underwear," Jane said.[1]

According to the Identity Theft and Assumption Act of 1998, identity theft (ID theft), occurs when someone is "knowingly transferring or using, without lawful authority, a means of identification of another person with the intent to commit, or to aid or abet, in the unlawful activity that constitutes a violation of federal law, or that constitutes a felony under any applicable state or local law."[2] It is a federal crime.

Still, ID theft is everywhere. This crime is committed when someone (often a con artist) gets access to a potential victim's personal information, such as date of birth, social security number, credit card numbers, PIN numbers, or driver's license. Much of this information can be easily obtained in a home mailbox, in home dumpsters, through theft, on the Internet, or through various other methods.

Identity theft targets young and old alike. It is in the metropolis and the small town. However, in the past few years it has taken its toll on many senior citizens, particularly in the Sun Belt states of Florida, California, Texas, and Arizona where affluent elderly with sufficient pensions or savings retire and escape the cold winters of northern states. More and more senior citizens suddenly discover that they have been "cloned" when bogus charges appear on credit card statements or on checks which they have not written and which are subtracted from their bank accounts. Although it does not indicate the number of identity theft cases prior to 2000, the American Association of Retired Persons reports "the number of cases has been doubling every year since [that time]."[3]

Some types of ID theft appear to be more popular than others. The *Rocky Mountain News* gave a breakdown of identity theft types as reported by Colorado victims in 2002. Credit card fraud was at the top of the list at 35 percent. In fact, a fairly new credit card scam has con artists asking victims for the three-digit card verification number that is printed on the back of the credit card in order to foil fraud. Apparently, con artists posing as legitimate VISA and Master Card employees state that they are calling from those companies' security and fraud departments. They indicate that they need the numbers to verify that the victims' cards have not been lost or stolen. The cons sound legitimate, even providing a "badge number" to lull their victims into a sense of security.[4] Because many people are aware of the possibility of ID theft, the victims are quick to comply with the caller's request.

Following identity theft with credit cards was bank fraud (at 21 percent) and phone/utilities fraud (at 19 percent). Identity theft was also reported in other categories, such as job-related incidents, consumer loans, and government documents or benefits fraud. Almost 25 percent of the victims reported more than one type of identity theft.[5] In other words, numerous incidents turned up in which their identities were being used fraudulently.

Although it doesn't usually make headlines or the early evening news, apparently every 79 seconds someone's identity is stolen in the United States. Statistics vary, but the numbers given certainly should get the public's attention. According to one source, this year more than 700,000 Americans (some sources put the figure at more than a million) will be robbed of their identities, with more than 4 billion dollars stolen in their names. Many of them will be senior citizens over the age of 65. Even federal regulators were surprised by a Federal Trade Commission (FTC) study of identity theft that turned up nearly 10 million victims and a loss of $53 billion for businesses and consumers in 2002. A more current study from the FTC released in September 2003 indicated there were 27.3 million victims in the past 5 years.[6]

Of course, anyone of any age can have his or her identity stolen, as was the case with 17-year-old Steven Rose, Jr. A close relative living in another state apparently had been using his name and social security number over a period of 6 years. Rose discovered the identity theft when he received a credit report indicating that he had delinquent payments amounting to over $30,000.[7]

However, many of those who report identity theft are senior citizens, or relatives of those elderly who have been bilked. A complaint filed with the FTC and cited in that organization's booklet on identity theft illustrates the problem many individuals face.

> My elderly parents are victims of credit fraud. We don't know what to do. Someone applied for credit cards in their name and charged nearly $20,000. Two of the card companies have cleared my parents' name, but the third has turned the account over to a collection agency. The agency doesn't believe Mom and Dad didn't authorize the account. What can we do to stop the debt collector?[8]

As the FTC indicates, obtaining legitimate identification or getting false identification appears to be so easy. Identity thieves get someone's personal information in a variety of ways: stealing wallets and purses, stealing mail, posing as an employer to obtain a credit report, obtaining personnel records at work, using personal information shared on the Internet, buying information from a clerk who may have access to a customer's financial information, or completing a change of address form to divert mail to another address. Another easy way to obtain someone's identity is to rummage through trash at their home, at their place of employment, or at any place where they do business. People are very careless about

discarding envelopes, sales slips, pay stubs, investment information, and similar documents. "Dumpster diving," as picking
through a trash receptacle is called, can provide easy access to all
kinds of information about a potential victim.

Without thinking, people daily toss unwanted items dealing
with finances into their trashcans at home, assuming that this is a
safe way to dispose of the huge amounts of paper or other debris
that tends to collect. After all, no one is going to cull through someone's dumpster sitting at the edge of their yard or business. Not so,
as one woman explained.

> This young woman who lived next door to me came to my back
> door one day last summer and asked if she could borrow a box of
> cake mix to make a cake for her husband's birthday. I must have
> looked puzzled at her request for she explained that she had looked
> in my trashcan and noticed an empty cake mix box. I couldn't
> believe what I was hearing. She had gone through my trash! Do
> people really do this?
>
> I didn't know what to say to her. I didn't know her at all well
> since I was usually at work and didn't see her often except as I was
> going in and out of my house. I did seem to know that she had sev-
> eral kids and didn't appear to have an awful lot of money. I think
> they rented, as the house always looked like it needed some repair
> and the yard wasn't kept up. But I wanted to be neighborly, so I got
> a cake mix from my shelves and handed it to her. But this gave me a
> really funny feeling . . . sort of like my privacy had been invaded.

Her privacy had been invaded, and from her trashcan a great
deal may have been learned about her lifestyle. Although the
above incident was apparently harmless regarding her financial
situation, this is not always the case. Some sales slips now only list
the last four digits of a customer's credit card number, but this is
not true in all instances. Those crumpled sales slips from grocery
and department stores may contain full credit card information
and, equally important, the card owner's signature, which may be
easy to duplicate. Stubs from monthly bills indicate the homeowner's name, address, and account number and often provide
information on the amount of credit still available. Letters from
credit card companies have account numbers printed at the top of
the correspondence, as well as attached blank checks just waiting
to be filled out, cashed, and charged to the victim.

Because most credit card bills show the types of merchandises or services purchased, these discarded items provide valuable information to con artists interested in offering their services to prospective victims. For example, if elderly homeowners bought paint for outside work, will they need a "cheap" paint contractor to help out? New carpets have been installed. Is a new vacuum cleaner warranted? The monthly mortgage payment is rather large. Would the homeowners be interested in refinancing? A partial hospital bill has been paid. Are "cheap" home care and medical supplies needed? An elderly person carelessly discarding trash may invite skillful con artists into their lives. An inexpensive shredder could help protect these seniors.

Every identifying number an individual possesses—social security, credit card, driver's license, telephone, cell phone—"is a key that unlocks some storage of money or goods," according to Bob Kuykendall, a fraud program manager of the U.S. Postal Inspections Service. "If someone gets access to a credit card receipt and uses the number on it, to Visa, American Express or any other credit card company, that individual becomes you—becomes your account. . . ."[9] Then that individual may be free to go on an unlimited shopping spree.

Of course, not all identity theft requires obtaining someone's lost or stolen credit card. For Grace W. (now incarcerated a second time) at an early age a little ingenuity made obtaining fake credit cards a fun game.

I had 42 identity cards, some stolen, a lot I made up. I first learned how easy it was to get false IDs when I was in high school—so that I could buy beer while still underage. Later on I found I could use fake IDs to support myself. It was like having a regular paycheck without having to hold a regular job.

Oh, sometimes, I would work for a short period of time as a clerk in department stores across the country—usually in the women's clothing department. When a customer made a purchase and gave me her credit card, I merely made a note of her name and the type of card she was using. Then I could call that credit card company, say I needed another card. If her name was Anne Jones, I usually said I needed the card for my daughter. For example, Marilyn Jones. I could give my employer, as I didn't expect to be working there long, and a fake social security number. Shortly the card would arrive at the address where I was living at that time, and I would sign for items as Marilyn Jones.

Occasionally, the store was running a special deal whereby the customer could get a discount if they filled out a credit application for a store card. That was really great as I had the women's address, phone number, social security number, age, etc. I was all set. I used these cards to buy things I wanted or needed and to cash checks at banks across the country.

Asked to give an approximate dollar amount gained for the years she had been using other people's identities, Grace thought for a minute and then said boastfully, "Oh, probably around $400,000, probably much more over the years. I lived pretty well as this was ongoing income. But I was very careful about where I lived, about who I talked to, and, of course, I moved around a lot."

Asked if this lifestyle wasn't a lonely one, she thought for a few minutes and then replied, "Well, yeah! I guess you could say that. I didn't have long-lasting friendships, if that's what you mean. But I'm the friendly type. I made acquaintances easily. You know, someone to run around with while I was in a town."

It is interesting to note that when Grace was finally apprehended, she was in a bank attempting to cash a check. Suddenly, she was aware of a great deal of commotion, with police accompanying the bank guard. Did she think that her scam had been discovered? No. "What I thought was, 'Oh, damn. Just my luck to be in this bank when someone decides to rob it.'"

Grace did not appear to be remorseful about her formerly illegal lifestyle nor the fact that she had cheated a great number of individuals and companies out of money. She further indicated that when she was finally released from prison in approximately 6 years, she would return to her "job" of stealing identities. "After all," she said smiling, "it took them [the police] several years to catch me. Maybe next time, I'll never get caught."

It would appear that Grace has a point. Identity thieves have found a myriad of ways in which to help themselves to the public's funds. Consider the plight of retired Air Force colonel John Stevens and his wife. Always prompt in taking care of his financial obligations, Stevens suddenly received a phone call from NationsBank inquiring as to why he was late on payments for a Jeep Cherokee which had been purchased in Dallas the previous year. Stevens protested that he had not been in Texas for 30 years and didn't have the jeep. Nevertheless, his name and social security number were on the contract for the automobile. In the months that followed, Stevens found that, using his credit, someone had purchased four more cars and other merchandise worth $113,000.[10] It took Stevens years of paper work to clear his name, and the culprit still remains a mystery.

Stevens was denied a loan to build a vacation home because of the glitch in his credit rating; some elderly persons have lost their homes due to ID theft. As many as 10 cases of fraudulent home sales have been investigated in the Detroit area and are called by privacy experts one of the most heartless kinds of identity theft. The perpetrators of this scam "locate houses in the metropolitan Detroit area that are owned free and clear by elderly people, assume the identity of the true owner, and strip the equity out of the houses without the true owner's knowledge or consent."[11]

Mildred K. and Eddie F. both suffered just such a loss when Jimmy Jones* and Eddie Reeves stole their identities, arranged fraudulent sales of or loans on the two Detroit houses, and pocketed the proceeds. Authorities said that Reeves posed as Millicent Barnett and, after presenting papers showing ownership of Mildred K.'s home, obtained a $99,000 mortgage on it. Jones was accused of posing as Eddie F. and, after presenting a fake Michigan driver's license for identification, ended up with a cashier's check for $99,805.36.[12] Neither of the victims was able to resolve the problem so that they could retain their property.

Of course not all of the dollar amounts stolen are as large as those of the above cases; however, it can be just as traumatic to the victim. Rebecca Sneddon found that someone had used her identity to charge over $3,000 in long-distance calls. Surprised to be turned down for loan because of bad credit, she obtained a copy of her credit record and discovered that an Illinois company had reported she was delinquent in paying $3,343 for phone calls. Upon checking further, she found that the telephone account was listed in her name at an address in Indio, California.[13] As is usually the case, Sneddon had never been to Indio nor did she know who could have been using her identity.

* Names have been changed in this section.

Another elderly woman, Maude A., was notified by her bank that nearly $2,500 in fraudulent checks had cleared her account in just a 2-day period. When she went to the bank, she saw that the checks had her account number but another person's name and address. Maude closed her account, took what little money was left in it, and got copies of each check. Still, there was little else she could do because she could not name any possible suspects.

One daughter saved her 80-year-old mother from sending money to LIFE, the Low Income Family Entitlement Program. An official-looking letter had advised her mother that she was entitled to $30,000 that would be paid in installments of $2,500. However, she was told, due to budget cuts, that the woman needed to pay $25 for processing her entitlement.[14] The biggest problem was not the $25 but the fact that in returning the fee, the woman needed to provide her social security number, date of birth, and a signature. This scam, which targeted the old and poor, provided all of the information necessary for identity theft.

A new twist on identity theft, recently found by Southern California law enforcement professionals, involves taking the scan card that opens a hotel guest's room. What people do not realize is that vital information is contained on that card key, such as name, partial address, credit card number, and so forth. Hotel employees have access to these cards after the guest returns them. The card keys are kept in an unlocked drawer; and the guest's personal information is not erased until the card is to be given to a new guest. An unscrupulous employee can steal the cards easily, take them home, and use a scanning device to access the information on a computer. The employees will then have an immense amount of credit available for quite some time as the victims involved usually are travelers who may not realize charges are not theirs. Some credit card companies randomly check customers' accounts, and if they see an unusually large number of charges coming from a state other than the cardholders' or a great deal of extra activity on the card, they will telephone the customers to verify if those charges are correct. However, most do not do this, so instead of returning the card key to the hotel desk clerk, it is best to take it along or cut it up.

Military personnel leaving the service are also being warned about recurring identity theft. Until recently those retiring were told that the local courthouse was a good place to store their DD Form

214. That was before the military services realized that, with a few exceptions, the form became a public record. Anyone wishing to do so could obtain the retirees' social security numbers and other personal data contained on the document.[15] Now, individuals are being urged to remove the document from local courthouses and store it in a safe deposit box or fireproof container at home.

What is very helpful to the identity thief, of course, is that most victims don't realize the theft occurred until months or sometimes years afterwards. The FTC indicated that "38 percent of all identity victims spend more than a month—and often much longer than that—to figure out what's happened to them."[16] Some indications that one may be a victim of this type of crime are failing to receive bills or other mail, which may be due to the address of the victim being changed by the identity thief; receiving credit cards which an individual did not request; being denied credit for no apparent reason; and receiving calls from collection agencies or companies about merchandise or services that the individual did not purchase.[17] All or any of these should alert people to the possibility that someone is using their identity.

PREVENTING IDENTITY THEFT

Sometimes it's difficult to realize that a person is being set up for identity theft. For example, one of the more imaginative tricks, which let thieves take advantage of a once-in-a-decade opportunity, was the United States Census. Jane S. Hoffman, New York City's commissioner of the Department of Consumer Affairs uncovered a scam whereby supposed census workers telephoned unsuspecting victims and requested a wide range of personal information, including social security numbers. If people demurred, they were transferred to a "supervisor" who repeated or verified the pitch.[18] Apparently, the elderly were primary targets because they were more likely to provide personal information in response to an insistent voice and because the person on the other end of the phone was calling from "the government." In instances like this, it is almost impossible to protect prospective victims.

Identity theft cases are so numerous that it is difficult for law enforcement to have enough manpower available to spend time trying to track down the thieves. According to a General Accounting Office report to Rep. Sam Johnson (R-Texas), it has not become a top crime-fighting priority, and some police departments may not be aware of the importance of taking reports of this crime, much less initiating investigations. Also, because identity theft cases tend to cross state and other jurisdictional lines, some law enforcement agencies may view these as being someone else's problem. Because of this, in November 2002, congressional and police groups adopted a resolution calling for "all law enforcement agencies . . . to take more positive action in recording all incidents of identity thefts."[19]

However, identity theft is not just the problem of law enforcement. The public needs to be reminded to do their part in helping to prevent this nontraditional but many times financially devastating crime. Tips to avoid becoming a victim are numerous. if not always easy to follow. For credit card safety the Department of Justice's *Consumer's Notebook* and AARP list the following.[20]

- Keep a list of credit card numbers, expiration dates, and phone numbers of credit card issuers in a safe place.

- Watch your credit card after giving it to a clerk and take it back promptly.

- Never sign a blank receipt.

- Write card issuers promptly to report any questionable charges.

- Avoid giving a credit card number over the telephone unless you have made the call. If you are called, do not give out this number unless you know the caller is trustworthy.

- Never write a credit card number on the outside of an envelope.

- Sign new cards immediately and destroy old cards. Cut up and return unwanted cards to the issuer.

- Report a lost or stolen card immediately by phone and with a follow-up letter.

- Guard personal information. Don't toss information pertaining to access codes, social security number, or credit card numbers in the trash. Shred these items.

- When choosing (or if given) PIN and ID numbers, do not make these easily available and try to see that they are not easily replicated.
- Shred all materials that have any form of identification on them. Inexpensive shredders can be purchased at almost all office supply stores as well as many other retail outlets. The key to shredding, however, is to use the machine once it is in the home.

If individuals think they've become victims of identity theft, they should act immediately to protect financial accounts, as well as their reputations. The California Public Interest Research Group (CalPIRG) and the Privacy Rights Clearinghouse list some actions to be taken.[21]

- Contact the FTC by mail, telephone, or online to report the situation.
- Contact the local office of the Postal Inspection Service to see if a change of address form has been submitted.
- Contact the Social Security Administration and the IRS in case identification information is being improperly used.
- Call the fraud units of the three major credit-reporting companies: Equifax, Experian, Trans Union.

In addition to the above, individuals may need to contact all creditors and notify them that identifying data may have been or is now being fraudulently used. Financial institutions where there are checking or savings accounts need to be contacted, and accounts may need to be cancelled or stop-payment orders placed on any outstanding checks. Change numbers on ATM cards and PIN numbers.[22]

A very good way for people to see if they may have been victims of fraud is to order a copy of their credit reports once a year from each of the three major credit bureaus—Trans Union, Equifax, and Experian. This is very important because fraud, and even mistakes, can wreak havoc with a person's finances. Many times victims of identity theft only discover that they have become victims when they attempt to make a major purchase, like a house or an automobile, and are turned down for bad credit. Regularly checking a credit report can prevent delays in completing these major transactions.

Balancing a checkbook each month also is critical, not only to check for fraud but to insure that no errors have occurred. Still, many elderly people cannot seem to find the time necessary to do this or simply find the chore too burdensome. As one semi-retired 65-year-old attorney said when this task was mentioned, "I never balance my checkbook. I just can't take the time." For whatever reason, those people who neglect this financial chore may become fair game for the identity thief and should take the time to make sure their finances are in order and kept safe.

Recently, with the number of identity thefts increasing, identity-theft protection services have become a growing industry with the services being sought by many. Promise-Mark, which offers a variety of services to protect possible victims, saw an upsurge of interest in 2002 after federal authorities arrested three men suspected of selling credit reports to street criminals. These reports, containing bank accounts, credit-card balances, and other personal information, helped drain millions of dollars from consumers across America. According to a study by the investment bank Stephens, identity-theft protection prices from specialized companies or reputable insurance agencies range from $29.95 to more than $100 a year.[23] However, there is a debate over whether these protection companies offer good value; some consumer advocates feel individuals can do as well by simply pulling their credit reports and checking them to see if they feel there are any discrepancies which might indicate identity theft—for example, credit cards that they have never requested.

Of course, there may be some things you shouldn't do, according to Mari Frank, an attorney and also an identity fraud victim. First, don't cancel all of your credit cards. Some may not be involved in the theft, and without cards you may be unable to buy groceries, rent a car, or make a hotel or sports event reservation. According to Frank, "Most of the time, someone is getting credit on a new account in your name . . . not putting charges on your [old] card because then you'd find out right away."[24] Although most people fail to do so, instituting a fraud alert will help in this instance.

Sometimes people hope that changing a social security number will free them from the identity thief, but this is not a good idea either, advises Frank. To do so may cause elderly individuals, who often have a long history of good credit, to lose this rating. If applying for credit, they may look suspicious to banks, lenders and even law enforcement agencies who will stumble across the old numbers when doing any kind of investigation.[25]

It would appear that preventing identity theft is a never-ending task; however, help is on the way. A financial services roundtable, representing 100 institutions handling about 70 percent of the economy's financial transactions, is in the process of creating an Identity Theft Assistance Center to help prevent identity theft. With this program, those who believe they are victims could call their bank, which in turn would call the assistance center. Then the center would collect an affidavit from the victim and send this to credit card companies, financial institutions, and law enforcement agencies.[26] Especially for the elderly, this would be a valuable service because they would have to make only one telephone call to report an incident, rather than contact all of their financial institutions individually.

There are also several other places to go which can be helpful. To learn how to restore your credit, contact the Federal Trade Commission, Consumer Response Center, 600 Pennsylvania Ave., N.W., Washington, D.C. 20580. For law enforcement help, contact the U.S. Postal Inspection Service or the U.S. Secret Service. (The telephone numbers are listed on the front pages of the local phone book.)

Chapter Five

Telemarketing Frauds

* * *

"Hello, Sucker!"
—Texas Guinan to nightclub patrons

* * *

At age 88, Janet Simpson was delighted when she received a telephone call indicating that she had won a new automobile. All she had to do was send a check to cover taxes and the cost of delivery. She did that. Shortly afterward she received another call asking for money to cover another charge. Janet sent another check and continued doing this until she had paid several thousand dollars and, of course, never did get a car.

At some point most citizens have received similar phone calls or a notice in the mail saying that a fabulous prize has been won or that, for an unbelievably small amount of money, they can have a dream vacation, a new car, a boat, or some other valuable item. A portion of these offers may be legitimate, but most are fraudulent. Although individuals would like to believe that they get lucky sometimes, common sense should tell them that seldom does anyone get something for nothing. Still, the Alliance Against Fraud in Telemarketing and Electronic Commerce reports that people age 60 and older accounted for 26 percent of telemarketing victims in 2001.[1] The National Fraud Information Center and the Department of Justice state that Americans lose approximately $40 billion each year due to the fraudulent sales of goods or services or in highly publicized sweepstakes. It is estimated that there are over 14,000 telemarketing firms conducting fraudulent telemarketing, with 43 percent of the victims over age 50 and 26 percent over age 60. The FBI found that fraudulent telemarketers directed nearly 80 percent of their calls at older consumers who have the time to talk and usually won't hang up. The repeated victimization of the elderly appears to be the cornerstone of illegal telemarketing and was listed third in 2002 among the top ten telemarketing frauds.[2]

The Web site of the National Fraud Information Center provided information on the top ten by percentage for January to June 2002. It is interesting to note that practically everyone with a telephone has been targeted by at least one of these. (Because they also arrive in mailboxes, some of these were discussed in Chapter 3.)

Credit card offers	27%
Work-at-home	21%
Prizes/Sweepstakes	15%
Advance fee loans	7%
Magazine sales	5%
Buyers clubs	4%
Telephone slamming	4%
Nigerian money offers	2%
Travel/Vacations	2%
Credit card loss protection	1%

The Web site also indicates that many of the victims are over age 70, and many of the telemarketers are located in California, Florida, Texas, New York, and Ontario, Canada.[3]

For the average citizen, it is often difficult to know the difference between reputable telemarketers and those who use the phone to perpetrate fraud. Many of these latter telemarketers are quite large and sophisticated fraud rings; others, of course, are merely seat-of-the-pants operations. All that is really required is a rented room, referred to as a boiler room, a number of telephones, and some experienced employees. Dishonest telemarketers are often pushy, urging the victims to act now because the offer won't be available later. They say a prize has been won, ask for a credit card number, or guarantee a "no-risk" investment. The telemarketer will have gotten names from a telephone directory, mailing list, or a "sucker list," which gives names of previously gullible victims. Now, everything is ready. Let the scams begin!

Sun Belt states are prime targets for telemarketing fraud because they have a growing population of senior citizens who have the assets that enable them to retire in a milder climate. Florida, Arizona, southern Texas, and southern California have been among the best hunting grounds for telemarketing schemes because these states have a large, affluent senior population. According to the National Consumers League, telemarketers often target the elderly as potential victims because they are more likely to have money, property, savings, and investments. They are also more likely to be at home to receive telephone solicitations and will remain on the phone longer because they may welcome someone who will let them tell their stories, talk about the weather, and inquire about their health.[4] Seniors are especially susceptible to scams offering prizes or various types of investment opportunities, asking for charitable donations, or assuring lottery winnings. Many elderly are so isolated that they seldom see family members, and many have outlived most of their friends, leaving them particularly vulnerable to anyone willing to give them a little time and companionship.

In one incidence a telemarketer was "clued in" to the fact that an elderly woman wanted her grandchildren to visit more often because she rarely got a chance to be with them. The telemarketer played on her emotions. He would send her presents on her birthday or some other special occasion. Then he would call back a few days later and ask if she received the package. After she had thanked him for the gift, he would ask what else she had received, guessing that she probably hadn't received any other gifts. After making these calls for some months, he then told the woman that he needed money. Because he had been so thoughtful, the old woman felt she couldn't turn him down.[5]

Many times the amount of money involved is tremendous. An elderly Ohio woman gave more than $240,000 to 50 fraudulent telemarketers. In California, a 92-year-old woman spent an original $180,000 and then over $5,000 in supposed recovery fees to a man who said he could get back some of her money. Another woman in her 70s was persuaded by a telemarketer to send $60,000, which came from her and her husband's retirement fund. When that money was gone, she was talked into taking out a loan for $13,000 more.[6] These women were victims of several types of scams, including lotteries, that appeal to all who believe they will have that lucky number.

THE CANADIAN LOTTERY

Want to make a great deal of money easily? Just call individuals listed in the telephone directory and indicate that they have won some tremendous amount of cash in a sweepstakes or lottery. Like Pavlov's dog, people begin to salivate as soon as they hear the words "cash" and "winnings" and, without thinking, are willing to do whatever is required to become suddenly wealthy. Although there are numerous sweepstakes scams, the Canadian lottery has been one of the biggest and most successful in recent years, hitting individuals in the U.S. and worldwide, both through the mail and, particularly, over the telephone.

An 83-year-old La Jolla, California, woman was more than willing to mail in two cashiers checks totaling $68,000 to pay for customs duties and taxes so that she could collect her $2 million Canadian lottery win. In 1999 an 81-year-old Los Angeles woman was presented with a bogus lottery check for $5.5 million and asked to pay $140,000 in taxes on her winnings. Alaska residents were contacted and informed that they had won $250,000 in a Canadian sweepstakes. To collect the money, they were instructed to send $2,500 in taxes and duties to a Western Union account in Quebec.[7]

Eighty-five-year-old Leah Larsen in San Luis Obispo was bilked out of at least $100,000 in one of the many Canadian telemarketing calls to that city. Another San Francisco Bay area woman, 70-year-old Rose Urbanski, who had been fleeced of $50,000 by Canadian con artists, was so embarrassed to tell her family she had fallen for the scam that she took a gun and committed suicide.[8] Although this is a rare case, the emotional and financial toll on victims can be profound, and individuals are continually being sucked in by promises of huge rewards. The number of victims taken in by the Canadian lottery con seem to be limitless in what the Royal Canadian Mounted Police (RCMP) have labeled an epidemic of telephone fraud. It certainly appears

to be an epidemic, as case histories like the one below number in
the thousands.

When Dan was 85 years old, he began receiving calls on a regular basis notifying him that he had won up to a million dollars in
the Canadian lottery. All he had to do to claim his winnings was to
send money to pay the required taxes. Shortly after he sent in a
check, another call would come saying a mistake had been made in
the amount needed and asking for more money. Dan always com-
plied with the request but, naturally, never received any of his winnings. His daughter Darlene said that he spent more than a million
dollars on various Canadian lottery entries until his death at age
88. Although his family had tried to convince him that the lottery
was a scam, he kept sending in tax money as directed. "Winning
became an obsession with him," Darlene stated.[9]

After Roy and Gladys sold their farm in 1996 for a fairly large
sum of money, their children were surprised to learn that the couple was $13,000 in debt. Upon investigating this, they discovered
that Roy had been sending out 50 to 100 checks a month to enter
sweepstakes and other contests. In one instance he had been told
that he could go to Montreal to pick up $125,000 because he was
included in a Canadian lawsuit to recover unpaid Canadian lottery
winnings. Canadian taxes that he was required to pay on his share
of the recovered money would be $4,000. Of course, there were no
recovered funds. Roy just assumed he was entitled to the $125,000
because he had previously sent $5,600 to pay taxes on other win-
nings that had never been received. "Not only did they scam him
into sending money the first time," explained his youngest son,
Charles, "but they further victimized him by playing on the fact
that he was a legitimate victim."[10]

Five North Carolina seniors, ages 71 through 86, recently
reported to the Consumer Fraud Task Force that representatives of
Mutual Financial Company called them to indicate that they had
won second place in a Canadian lottery. They were instructed to
send a cashier's check for $4,900 to pay the courier's "bonding fee"
so that their $300,000 in winnings could be released. They were
told to keep their winning confidential and not to contact anyone
regarding the boon because the matter was very "hush-hush."[11] In
this instance some vague threats were made to get compliance.
Participants were warned not to talk or something might happen

to them, and one of the targets who balked at sending money was told that someone would come and "get her."

Gloria Vettor, who consistently won bingo jackpots and was considered by family and friends to be very lucky, was not surprised when a Montreal company called to say she had won $50,000 in a sweepstakes. After all, she was used to winning. Although Vettor could not remember entering the contest and did not have the $2,140 requested to cover fees, she "borrowed" the money from her employer by forging checks to herself in his name. Over the next few months, Vettor was called by her new telephone friends to say that her winnings had now increased to $2.7 million and continued to embezzle funds to cover the charges necessary to retrieve her newly won fortune.[12] Naturally, no pot of gold was forthcoming—only a 2-year prison sentence on three counts of embezzling. Apparently, Vettor never became suspicious as the scam progressed and accepted amazing excuses as the reason for the numerous delays in getting her sweepstakes winnings.

For 85-year-old Drusilla Aden from Chicago, $13 million was to be her windfall from a Canadian lottery. However, there was a catch. Because she was a U.S. resident, she had to pay $1.8 million in taxes to collect her winnings. Immediately, Aden cashed in stocks and sent one check, then several others in the following months amounting to a total of $1,377,000 in Canadian funds. Investigators eventually were called in, but Aden still was loath to admit that she had been scammed.[13] In Aden's case a 29-year-old man was charged with fraud, but it was too late to retrieve all but a small portion of Aden's money.

Jane Feather, a task force member of the Consumer Protection Section of North Carolina's Division of Aging, received a report from a family that their elderly mother had been taken by a variation of the lottery fraud—the Canadian Barrister Scam. First, a man purporting to be a Canadian barrister (lawyer) informed the senior citizen that she would be receiving a prize of $300,000. Two days later another man called and instructed her to go to the Bi-Lo Supermarket and, through the Western Union facility there, wire $11,000 to Tel Aviv in order to pay the required taxes on her windfall. The elderly mother paid the "taxes" plus approximately $470 in wire transfer fees.[14] There is a saying, "You can't win the lottery unless you buy a ticket." Yet, in all of these cases, none of the victims appeared to be suspicious of winning a lottery that they had not entered.

Also, it must be assumed that none of those tricked were aware that participating in a foreign lottery, either through the mail or over the telephone, is in violation of a federal law. In September 2002, the FTC filed a complaint in U.S. district court in Chicago charging that a group of 14 Canadians was operating telemarketing boiler rooms in an illegal foreign lottery scheme that targeted American seniors. As with all of these scams, the telemarketers told the consumers that they had a good chance of winning the lottery or that they had already won a large prize and to send money to redeem the winnings. The FTC indicated that these claims were not only deceptive but that they violated the FTC Act and the Telemarketing Sales Rule.

> In October 2002, the court issued a temporary restraining order and barred the defendants from selling tickets, chances or any foreign lottery chances to residents of the United States; barred deceptive claims about the chances of winning the Canadian lottery; prohibited misrepresentations or commission about material facts; and ordered an asset freeze to preserve funds for consumer redress.[15]

Not all of the defendants agreed to abide by the injunction, and this one court case does not include all of the boiler rooms still offering consumers the opportunity to be fleeced. Many individuals hoping to win the pot of gold at the end of the rainbow will continue to contribute large sums of money to the Canadian lottery fraud.

FRAUDULENT MAGAZINE SUBSCRIPTIONS

Almost everyone who has a telephone at one time or another has received a call soliciting subscriptions to magazines. Many elderly select and subscribe to a number of weekly or monthly magazines, ones that they desire to read. However, often they are the target of telemarketers who use various methods to cajole the unsuspecting into taking additional subscriptions. The FTC uncovered (and prosecuted) a scheme in which senior citizens were lured into paying hundreds of dollars, not just for yearly subscriptions but for multi-year subscriptions.[16] Apparently, the telemarketers were able to convince the victims that they were only entering a sweepstakes contest. Often they were assured that the magazines were free, that they only had to pay shipping and handling, and that they could cancel at any time. However, even if the first few mailings were free, many seniors failed to return notices indicating that they wished cancellation and were stuck with the subscriptions.

Even when calling to order products from a company, individuals many times are given a pitch about magazines. "Because you are a valued customer, today we have a special offer for you," the honeyed voice of the salesperson explains at the end of the catalog order. "We will send you free of charge for 3 months your choice of four magazines. There is no obligation on your part, and you can cancel at any time." After that, a list of the available magazines is recited and the "free" offer is emphasized. Again, the catch is that most subscribers hear the word *free* and pay no attention to the limitation of 3 months before cancellation is due. They usually forget to cancel. The magazines keep coming, along with a bill that most people feel obligated to pay since they received the merchandise.

CHARITY CALLS

Americans like to feel that they are charitable people who are willing to help those less fortunate than themselves. Most of these Americans will, at one time or another (and particularly around the Christmas holidays) receive a plea through the mail (Chapter 3) or from a telemarketer asking for a charitable contribution; most will decide to send some amount of money to help those in need. Telemarketers have found many Americans sympathetic to the tales of hungry children in third-world countries or victims of natural disasters around the world.

Since the September 11, 2001, attack on the World Trade Center, charitable contributions have been widely solicited to help victims' families and to support police and firefighters. Many times the call purportedly comes from a police or fire service organization; however, donors should be cautious because simply having the words "firefighter" or "police" in an organization's name doesn't mean police or firefighters are members of the group or are even soliciting funds. Inquiring if the individual calling is employed in one of these occupations or if the call is from a local law enforcement agency will often result in the telemarketer disconnecting the call.

Generally, telemarketers (like appeals in the mail) give the impression that all donations are used for charity and are reticent when questioned about the exact amount the charity will receive. The public assumes that most of its donation is going to those in need, but consumer attorney Alan Kopit (of NBC News) indicated that studies show seniors are less likely to know how their donations to a charity are being spent.[17] Those making donations are constantly being warned in the media to be wary because sometimes only 10 percent of a donation actually reaches the charity. Many telemarketers are helping themselves instead of the needy.

Obviously, telemarketing is a business, and, like any business, those collecting for charity have overhead costs and employees to pay. However, if a telemarketing firm solicits money for charities, keeps most of the funds it raises, and misleads potential donors about this fact, the U.S. Supreme Court ruled in May 2003 that states can prosecute the telemarketer for fraud. This decision was the result of the Illinois attorney general filing fraud charges against an Illinois telemarketer whose contract with a veterans' charity, VietNow, allowed it to keep 85 percent of the donations it raised.[18] Originally, the state court had ruled that the percentage kept by the telemarketing firm was not, by itself, evidence of fraud, and the case moved up to the Supreme Court. In addition, "AARP filed a friend of the court brief in the case, focusing on the scope of telemarketing fraud and its impact on older people who are frequent targets of phone scams."[19]

In order not to contribute to a group that misrepresents its fundraising activities, people should ask for the charity's full name and address and whether it is licensed by state and local authorities, although licensing does not necessarily imply endorsement. (Some states require a registration number.) Ask if professional solicitors are hired and paid to make the solicitation and, if so, what percentage of the donations go to the solicitor. It is also wise to inquire about the name of the telemarketing company that employs the paid solicitor and the location of this company. If in doubt about the authenticity of the telemarketer, ask for printed material. (One man indicated that he always does this so that he can take time to evaluate the requests for money.) Beware of appeals for contributions that resemble an invoice or statement of money due. These should bear a disclaimer stating that it is only an appeal, not an obligation to pay. Don't send cash, and always ask if the contribution is tax deductible. If in doubt about the charity, check with local law enforcement or the Better Business Bureau before giving way to a charitable inclination and sending in a donation. Also, check to see if the charity has a local facility or a direct mailing address. If individuals would like to donate, most charities will accept direct donations, so they should go there and make a direct contribution.

TRAVEL FRAUD

Scams that have to do with travel are constantly bilking citizens who fall for tantalizing calls that seduce them to "get away from it all." Today, many retired couples can afford the luxury of traveling to major cities, national parks, or exotic ports around the world. Frequently, they may be tempted at trade shows, craft fairs, restaurants, or shopping malls to sign up to win a "free" trip. Shortly after, the couples may receive notification in the mail or hear a voice on their telephone saying, "Congratulations! You have won a luxury dream vacation"—to Mardi Gras, Hawaii, England, Tahiti, or other exotic locations. Watch it! Generally this is known as a "trip trap."[20]

As with other offers, some travel opportunities sold over the phone are legitimate; however, many are scams that defraud consumers out of millions of dollars each year. Chances are the "free" trip that was won isn't free, and the luxury accommodations on a cruise ship may turn out to be similar to old-fashioned steerage. The telemarketer may ask for a credit card number to cover minor costs not covered by the free package. Then, receiving the details of the travel package may entail another fee. Many offers also conceal hidden costs—port charges, service fees, hotel taxes, fees for a tour guide, airfare to and from a port of embarkation for a cruise, tips, and other costs. New charges continue to be added until the free trip costs more than it would if the customers had gone to a reputable travel agency for their vacation package.

Also, if told that the trip can be taken any time within 18 months, be careful. Promising that bargain prices to a desirable location are always available may not be true because both prices and availability of accommodations vary between peak and off-season times. In addition, if consumers wait too long to take advantage of a special tour, the company may have gone out of business before the deal can be fulfilled.

An excellent example of this was Catherine, age 66, who won a Caribbean cruise—all expenses paid. All she had to do was forward $200 to cover the minimal charges of port taxes, airline taxes, and hotel taxes. As soon as her check cleared the bank, she was told that her tickets would be forthcoming. Finally, after the tickets failed to arrive, she was informed by a friend, who was a magazine editor, that her awaited cruise was simply a travel scam.[21]

Despite a slump in the travel industry, travel fraud appears to be booming. In 2002, the FTC indicated that over three thousand consumers reported losing $3.5 million in various vacation scams. Retirees Sandra and James Wentworth of Illinois are just one example of those who purchase memberships in travel clubs. The Wentworths paid Travel More Now of Branson, Missouri $7500 for membership and the club's advertised "lifelong discounts." Hoping to get a steep discount on a trip to Niagara Falls, the Wentworths contacted the club and were booked into a hotel 25 miles from the falls at $57 a night. When they went online, they discovered there were hotels by the Falls for half the price. Sandra Wentworth contacted the travel club for a refund but received no results. "It's a nightmare," she said, "It has worn me out trying to get them to do anything for us."[22]

Midwest Marketing contacted people and informed them that they were "guaranteed winners" of at least one of five prizes: a Mazda Miata, $5,000 in cash, five dream vacations, a home entertainment center, or $1,000 in cash. To receive these prizes, the winners would have to pay for promotional fees and taxes. The average amount requested (and usually paid)[23] for the vacation package was $249.49. However, Midwest Marketing purchased the actual packages for $45 from a company called Premium Research, whose business was selling various items and packages to telemarketers. A few of the people who sent money received a vacation voucher; however, some received only a "gimmie gift" of a cheap bracelet, and most received nothing at all. Still, the lure of winning a vacation to some faraway place is too tempting to resist.

Another of the major problems with travel is that many companies offering special deals, tour packages or the ability to win a trip have gone out of business, leaving the traveler with little recourse to recoup losses. For the last 15 years consumer protection has been available through the National Tour Association (NTA), which represented about 640 tour companies. In 2002 the NTA paid out $565,000 in refunds to customers of six NTA member firms that went bankrupt. However, the NTA has given warning that it will no longer provide such protection to travelers for tours that begin on or after January 1, 2004. The reason for canceling this protection is that it has become "far too expensive," according to NTA President Hank Phillips.[24] Of course, travel companies with legitimate packages can go bankrupt; however, legal or illegal, the consumer is still the loser if bankruptcy occurs.

There are a couple safeguards seniors might consider before booking tours, joining travel clubs, or entering lotteries to win free trips. First, pay with a credit card. "Under the Fair Credit Billing Act, credit card customers can, within certain time limits, obtain refunds for goods and services they never received."[25] Travel insurance to provide protection against cancelled or delayed trips (and possibly bankruptcy) is another option. Whether purchasing insurance or signing up for a tour, reading the fine print is a necessity.

A PLETHORA OF SCAMS

There seem to be no end to the types of telemarketing calls that lure senior citizens to financial doom, and rip-offs dealing with medical costs are on the rise. One woman received a call from a man who said he was associated with Medicare. During a friendly chat, the man asked the woman about her medical supplies and whether her suppliers were doing what they were supposed to do. Then he explained that he could get her medicine sent directly to her if she wished. Thinking she was speaking with a Medicare representative, the woman provided the con artist with both her husband's and her social security numbers. It was fortunate that the woman mentioned the incident to her daughter, who reported it to the police. "This is the same lady who shreds all of her mail because she's aware of identity theft," a police officer explained. "[But] When someone says 'Medicare' and 'health insurance' and 'benefits,' these elderly people get scared. That's [a] scammer's way of terrifying these people."[26] The police officer made a good point. Seniors tend to respond quickly to any call that is supposedly from an official agency. Since medical treatment is so expensive, they are dependent upon Medicare and other health insurance, and the thought of possible problems with this protection elicits an immediate response.

Hearing from a smooth-talking telemarketer that medical discount cards were available to provide huge savings lured in people such as Dorothea Papandrea, a retired chef on Long Island. The card, at a cost of $340 annually, was purported to generate savings on everything from drugs to vision care, with a 30-day money back guarantee if she were not satisfied. However, the discounts were so minimal that Papandrea found she would not even recoup her annual fee. When she asked for her refund, Toronto-based MedPlan, Inc. refused. Before Canadian and U.S. law enforcement authorities moved to freeze its assets and shut it down in 2002, MedPlan, Inc. had raked in $8 million. Some of the seniors caught up in this scam thought they had purchased insurance for hospitalization. However, when they walked into hospitals with their discount cards, they found they hadn't purchased insurance. "When they're hit with the bill," says Kim Streit of the Florida Hospital Association, "they don't have the resources to pay."[27] All too often older people, desperate to obtain some form of medical coverage and, particularly, a discount on prescription drugs, fall for this type of fraud.

An elderly victim was nearly caught by another common scam known as the One in Four (or Five, Six, and so on) Scheme, the number of prizes offered differing with each fraud. First, the man received a letter informing him that he had won one of four different prizes, with the top prize being a Cadillac Seville valued at $42,000, plus $50,000 in cash. Later a telemarketer called and explained that he had won the top prize and that he would be interviewed on NBC. Then, after a few more days had passed, a man named Lance called and said the car would be delivered via the International Relief Fund, and, because of this, there would be a brokerage fee of $6481.16 to be paid to a brokerage firm known as Genmark.[28] Luckily, this targeted mark decided not to send the money to Lance, who is apparently a former Canadian actor and well-known to law enforcement officials.

In another scam, a Canadian operation (different from the lottery fraud and eventually shut down by the Royal Canadian Mounted Police) sold phony British bonds to hundreds of American seniors.[29] This Vancouver, British Columbia boiler room targeted gullible individuals looking for a quick profit and whose names appeared on a "sucker list" of those previously ripped off in other telemarketing schemes.

Offers to purchase protection against loss of a credit card also are popular scams among fraudulent promoters. One woman recalls a call from a female telemarketer, "She said I needed credit card loss protection insurance. I have gotten more forgetful or careless the older I get and am always misplacing my credit cards, so I decided to listen to what she was saying. I told her that I thought there was a law that limited my liability to $50 for unauthorized charges in case of card loss. But she said the law had been changed and that now, people were liable for all unauthorized charges on their account, no matter how much that was."[30] The pitch was not true. Credit card loss insurance protection programs are worthless. Those companies issuing credit cards have procedures for disputing unauthorized charges, and, according to the FTC, the owner of the card is limited to paying $50 for charges they didn't make. However, this victim purchased the insurance because she believed the telemarketer who indicated that she was only trying to protect the woman from possible financial loss.

ONCE A VICTIM, ALWAYS A VICTIM?

Like those seniors targeted to purchase the phony British bonds, it is not uncommon for telemarketing schemes to burn the victims twice by taking their money and then selling the names of these "suckers" to other fraudulent telemarketing operations. Taking advantage of a television offer which turns out to be less than satisfactory may result in telephone calls regarding similar products available for purchase Elderly individuals commonly have received five or more calls a day from high-pressure telephone salespeople once they have succumbed to previous calls.[31] After individuals fall for various scams a number of times, their names may end up on what is known as a "sucker list" or a "mooch list."[32] Fraudulent telemarketers often network with each other and mail, fax, or e-mail lists of suckers names to other con artists, an invaluable tool for swindlers.

Many individuals who were susceptible to the original con artists' sales spiels, sadly, become victims a second time. In what is known as the "reload," successful fraud operators often make an attempt to gain even more. For example, in a typical reload, the con artist again contacts the victim and either builds up the original scam by adding a new twist to it or pitches a completely new scheme.[33] When the marks take the bait, they are stripped of additional money. Apparently, the old adage "once bitten, twice shy" does not apply to a fair number of senior citizens.

From the mooch or sucker lists, scam operators contact those who have lost money to a previous telemarketing scam and promise that, for a fee, they will recover the lost money. To add to their credibility, these "recovery room" operators use a variety of misrepresentations. Their pitch may be that they represent companies or government agencies, that they are holding money for the victim, that they will file a complaint with government agencies on the victim's behalf, or that they can get a victim placed at the top of a list for victim reimbursement.[34] All of these claims turn out to be false, and the second-time victim is out the additional funds paid to the recovery room telemarketer.

Capitalizing on the popularity of existing state Do Not Call lists, con artists have devised a clever method to get consumers to part with personal information. They claim that they are not calling to sell anything but are providing a service because the consumers have signed up on a Do Not Call list. Basically, this is how the con artist operates: An individual will call, usually claiming to represent a Do Not Call registry or the FTC, and ask the senior citizens to verify that they are on the list by giving out their social security number or a credit card number.[35] All of this sounds like an official government call, but once the personal information is made available, the con artist is free to run up debts or steal the identity of the seniors.

Recently, the New York State Protection Board uncovered a scheme whereby a telemarketing organization was selling victims "protection" against telemarketing fraud. Among these was the

Senior Advisory Council, based in Phoenix, that offered buyers protection against a Toronto-based group, Consumer Alliance, which had victimized thousands of people across the United States. Originally, buyers paid Consumer Alliance $350 for a fraudulent credit card "protection plan" that consisted of nothing but brochures and stickers for avoiding pitfalls. For these victims caught in the $350 plan, the Senior Advisory Council was now providing a $247 offer to protect them against more scams, sometimes mentioning Consumer Alliance by name.[36] However, this new telemarketing "protection package" provided almost no security to the buyer and, basically, was just another scam.

In a similar rip-off, telemarketers told consumers that their personal and financial information was "all over the Internet" and on various other marketing lists. For a fee, the callers said they could remove this information. Sometimes stating that they represented a bank, they asked for the consumers' bank account, credit card, and social security numbers. Usually the telemarketers would not take no for an answer and would intimidate their victims by harassing them, using abusive language, calling them repeatedly, and bullying them. (One woman hung up on a telemarketer who immediately called her back and warned her not to hang up again.) The FTC found that this telemarketing group used at least three different aliases: Peace and Quiet, R&R Consultants, and the Consumer Alert Agency.[37] Probably operating from boiler rooms and moving to a new location every few weeks, con games such as this are well-orchestrated and almost impossible to locate and prosecute by law enforcement agencies.

Of course, occasionally a person is able to recoup losses from a pushy telemarketer. After being pressured to purchase "needed" credit card insurance, Anna B. finally mailed in a check for $100. When she mentioned the purchase to her daughter, that woman became suspicious and urged her mother to call her local bank about the purchase. When Anna was informed that she didn't need the insurance, she immediately called and cancelled the policy. However, it took repeated calls to the telemarketing phone number before she was finally reimbursed. Still, Anna was fortunate that she could reach the company. Most of the boiler rooms have their original phones disconnected after a few weeks of calling in an area and replace them with new phones and numbers.

HANG UP!

Although the FTC's telemarketing sales rule has been that telemarketers should not call before 8:00 A.M. or after 9:00 P.M.,[38] some continue to do so. Because most people are taught to be polite when called on the phone, they listen to the information pouring out of the earpiece. To avoid being disturbed by a call or falling for a scam, the best advice is to simply hang up or just say no. However, this is difficult for many who try to be polite, and telemarketers can be persistent. An Army wife who sold credit cards as a telemarketer stated that even if the victim was brusque or rude to her, she still was required by the company to try three times to get the person to say yes. She had scripted rebuttals when those she called tried to refuse. If people indicated they were not interested, she would ask how they could say that if they didn't know what she was selling. If they said it was too expensive, she would reply that the card cost them nothing. If they didn't need more credit cards, she would encourage them to pay off their other cards with the new one she was hawking.[39]

However, even Alicia admitted that she had qualms about her job. "It got to be so stressful calling 80- and 90-year-old men and women who couldn't even get out of their beds to shop with a credit card," she stated. "I went home and cried at the end of the day."[40] Those receiving calls can always tell the telemarketer to stop calling, and once telemarketers have been requested to do so, they should honor this request. However, the best bet for individuals may be to get the name of the company calling and tell them to remove their names from the company's calling list. If they fail to do so and call again, people can complain to the FTC.

The National Do Not Call Registry offers a great deal of protection from fraud *if* people will register for this list. When the FTC rule was proposed in 2002, more than 43,000 responses appeared on the FTC's Web site—most favoring the national registry and commenting "Do it, and do it now."[41] While many individuals have registered on the list, there are still many who have not done so.

For those who have access to the Internet, the FTC has a guide online to help protect consumers from both inbound and outbound calls. It lists the telemarketing sales rule (in effect since December 31, 1995); the Telephone Consumer Protection Act (TCPA), which imposes restrictions on the use of auto dialers; the mail or telephone order merchandise rule (enacted in 1975 and enforced by the FTC); and the 900-number rule (in effect since November 1993), which delivers information or entertainment programs over the phone and bills the caller's phone. Information is listed on where to complain and get help if individuals feel they have been victims of a scam, wish to dispute a credit card charge, or report violations of the Do Not Call list.[42]

Still, the telemarketing sales rule does not cover all calls, including calls seeking charitable donations, catalog sales, calls placed by consumers in response to direct mail advertising *if* the advertising discloses information required by the rule, sales of pay-per-call services and sales of franchises.[43] Citizens must take some responsibility for their own protection against telemarketing fraud. The National Consumers League's National Fraud Information Center offers some good advice.[44]

- Know whom you're dealing with.
- Don't believe promises of easy money.
- Think twice before entering contests operated by unfamiliar companies.
- Guard your personal information.
- Beware of bogus recovery services.
- Report violations.

However, when individuals are not certain that the friendly voice on their phones is legitimate, don't feel pressured. There is always one option. Hang up!

Chapter Six

Caretakers and Crime

Widowed, mentally or physically incapacitated, alone and fearful! All or any of these situations face America's growing elderly population. In general, society assumes that there will be someone who will take care of the elderly in an honest and caring fashion. However, often this is not the case. Children, grandchildren, other relatives, financial advisors and those staff in assisted living or nursing facilities often take financial advantage of frail or mentally incapacitated men and women. "This was my daughter," a 78-year-old woman explained, wiping away tears that had begun to trickle down her cheeks. "My daughter. The daughter who I raised, loved. I gave her a lot of money, but I only have a small pension and a bit in savings. Then she advised me to invest some money in the stock market for a better interest rate. When I agreed, she took my savings bonds and cashed them and kept the money for herself. She stole from me—my daughter. I thought she cared about me; I was fooled."

This case is not unique. Although everyone would like to believe that relatives, friends and even hired help will always be honest and caring, this is far from reality. When money is involved, love and loyalty by children often fades away, and unscrupulous caregivers are always looking for a way to dupe the older individual.

It is no secret that people are living longer. By 2040 nearly 21 percent of Americans will be elderly, and sociologists now have two categories for these individuals. Those between the age of 65 and 74 are the "young old"; those 85 and older are the "old old."[1] According to another demographic from a study from AARP, in 2002 nearly 44 percent of Americans in their fifties had at least one parent alive who needed some type of care. More and more those Americans in the 50-plus age group are joining a fast-growing corps of children who find they must take on the physical and financial responsibility for parents and other older relatives or rely on some kind of hired assistance.[2] Either way, they can encounter a myriad of problems as they attempt to live up to their filial responsibilities.

Dealing with a parent's or relative's financial situation isn't easy as the caregiver will find that retirement finances can be fairly complicated for those elderly who have even modest amounts of assets. Susan Herman, director of the National Center for Victims of Crime, also emphasized that seniors may be reluctant to confront the idea that they need this help as they fear "they will no longer be considered competent to handle their own financial affairs."[3] They may view this change in their lives as a sign that they are no longer considered adults and, like children, must have help. Therefore, although most seniors resist giving up control over their money, they eventually may need to place additional names on property deeds, to give access to credit cards or bank accounts, or to sign a power of attorney.

THE POWER OF ATTORNEY:
LICENSE TO STEAL

Probably the most dangerous action anyone can take is giving a power of attorney to another person. Of course, when an individual is incapacitated, someone has to take responsibility to pay household bills, make mortgage payments, cover medical costs, and take care of many other financial matters. The General Durable Power of Attorney is just what it says—it gives the following authority by the principal to the agent whose name is listed on the document.

> My agent may do everything necessary in my name and for my benefit which I could do if I were personally present and able. It is my intention that my agent may perform any act and exercise any power, duty, right or obligation that I could perform or exercise. Such authority is intended to relate to any person, transaction or interest concerning real and personal property, including tangible property interests, in which I now have an interest, and property in which my interest is subsequently acquired. I empower my agent to delegate authority to others.
>
> The following powers are illustrative of my agent's authority; they are not intended to be exclusive:
>
> 1. To acquire, encumber and dispose of any interest of mine in real or personal property upon such terms as my agent determines to be appropriate.
> 2. To hold, invest, lease and otherwise manage any interest of mine in real or personal property; to recover possession of property by lawful means; and to maintain, protect, insure, move, store, report, rebuild, alter, or improve any of that property.
> 3. To transact every kind of business including the collection, payment, and settlement of all amounts and interests receivable by me or payable by me or to me.
> 4. To make, endorse, execute, deliver and receive deed . . . drafts, notes, receipts.

In addition to the above, the power of attorney also gives the agent full authority to withdraw money from the individual's bank or similar institution, to borrow "in my name for my benefit," to have access to any safe deposit boxes, and to transfer property. What may be of more importance than monetary concerns is the power given to the agent to act on behalf of the individual signing the document in "consenting to or refusing medical treatment." This general power of attorney does not terminate and survives until the principal's death or until the maker has it revoked.[4]

Usually a trusted family member or close caregiver is authorized to hold the power of attorney, and, usually, this individual handles the principal's affairs in an orderly and conscientious manner, taking into consideration all family members who may share in any inheritance upon the demise of the incapacitated individual. However, an unscrupulous family member can take advantage of the other heirs, as was the case related by Monica.

> Without telling us that she had done this, my 83-year-old mother gave power of attorney to my brother. He was the oldest of us five kids. I don't know if she did this willingly or if he talked her into it. She was still living in her home, the family home, when she did this. It was not a palace, but it was a nice home, and she had nice furniture. She also had a fairly new automobile and quite a bit of savings.
>
> When mom became ill and had to have an operation, Tom had her moved to a nursing home after the surgery for convalescence and just never took her home. She lived about 10 months, and all of us visited her often. Even though some of us lived quite far away, we managed to get to the home and see if she was getting good care. Of course, Tom lived right there in town.
>
> Mom never said anything about the power of attorney but did mention that she had a will. Still, when she died we learned that Tom had already sold her house while she was in the nursing home, that he had cleaned out all of her bank accounts, had cashed in what little stock she had, and that was that. We contacted an attorney, but he told us there was nothing we could do. Since Tom had the power of attorney, he could dispose of anything of hers. It didn't matter about the will, which divided the property and money between all five of us. There wasn't anything left to divide. He had already taken it all. The rest of us were left out in the cold. We just couldn't believe our brother would do this to us, but he did.

Caregivers other than those related by blood also may be able to obtain a power of attorney from an unsuspecting victim by convincing them that they will provide needed care. A classic case is that of Alice J. who, after her husband's death, relied on a son's friends for much of her care. Alice suffered from a variety of illnesses, including retinopathy (loss of eyesight due to diabetes), and had need of help with all of her affairs. Alice was not on good terms with either her daughter or son, but she had met her son's friend Joan, who had been extremely friendly and had spent quite a bit of time visiting Alice. Joan offered to take on the role of caregiver and to ensure that all of Alice's finances were kept in order.

Everything seemed to be running smoothly until a neighbor, who had become good friends with Alice and her late husband, received a call from Alice's daughter in California indicating that she had discovered that her mother had loaned $40,000 to Joan and her husband, Flip. The daughter further stated that the $40,000 had been part of a $60,000 settlement from her father's life insurance policy. When she questioned her mother about the loan, Alice had been quite explicit about the daughter minding her own business. The daughter also said that her mother explained that Joan and Flip were good people. In fact the mother said that she had nick-named the man Flipper, and would tease him about this. She added that he liked the nickname and always laughed with her.

No security had been given for the money loaned nor had a contract been signed, and the daughter wanted the neighbor to see if there was a way to secure the debt owed to her mother by Joan and Flip. Although somewhat hesitant to do so, the neighbor did as requested and was able to secure a written contract between all parties acknowledging the $40,000 debt and the assurance that the additional $20,000 would only be utilized as an emergency fund for Alice and would not otherwise be touched. Joan and Flip also agreed to begin repaying Alice in July of 1999.

Then, in January 2002, the neighbor noticed workmen measuring the outside of Alice's home. When he questioned them, he discovered that the purpose for the activity was to obtain an appraisal of the house and property so that Alice could apply for a mortgage. At that time he talked with Alice's mother and was able to ascertain that she was deeply in debt, behind on her monthly bills, and requesting a mortgage for $30,000.

The neighbor then contacted Alice's daughter who asked him to get in touch with Joan and Flip to learn the circumstances for the mortgage. Although Joan agreed to a meeting, she pleaded a tooth-ache and failed to show up. When the neighbor again spoke with his elderly friend, he found that Joan had talked Alice into going ahead with the mortgage because she and Flip were going to lose their house due to failure to make their mortgage payments. If that happened, Alice said that the couple had warned her that they were leaving town and "she would be completely alone with no one to care for her." The neighbor became even more concerned and questioned Alice further about her finances.

I asked her what had happened to the $20,000 in reserve from the $60,000 policy, and she said that Joan told her it was all gone. She had not questioned Joan about why or where the money had been spent as she didn't want Joan and Flip to stop taking care of her. She also informed me that Joan had her checkbook and credit cards, had her power of attorney, and that Joan's name was on all of her accounts and had been since shortly after her husband died.

Immediately, I assisted Alice in having the power of attorney withdrawn. Still, all kinds of financial problems surfaced. Alice only had $130 in her credit union account; there had been $8,000 in a savings account. Only $500 of this had been used to open an account in both Alice's and Joan's names. The remainder of the money—all $7,500—had just disappeared. Of an additional $59,000 which had been in certificates of deposit or money market accounts, only $4,000 remained. I was told by bank employees that Alice never came in to withdraw money; however, Joan was in several times a month. Although they had been suspicious, there was nothing they could (or should) do as Joan's name was on the account.

Another pattern of fraud began to emerge. Joan and Flip had paid back the $40,000 they borrowed from Alice but had done this by withdrawing the $59,000 in Alice's savings. What happened to the extra money was never known. I also found evidence that even before Alice's husband had died, he had kept records of loans that he also had made to Joan and Flip in the amount of $11,000.

In addition to all the loans, there were credit card debts to Sears in the amount of $10,000, J.C. Penney for $920, the Prescription Shop for $1200, Texaco for $900, and numerous others. I also found that there had been two separate loans made in Alice's name by US Bank of which she had no knowledge. Joan apparently made these loans using Alice's power of attorney.

All in all, the neighbor believed that the amount taken from Alice during a period of approximately 3 years was well over $100,000. Joan and Flip are no longer living at their home and left no forwarding address. Fortunately, Alice still has the help of her neighbor and has reconciled with her son and daughter who are also involved in trying to assist her.

Sometimes a person becomes inadvertently involved in a power of attorney situation. Susan P. of Boise, Idaho, was an active 69-year-old who had married John 10 years prior. Both had grown children from previous marriages who lived out of state. When Susan fell and broke her hip, her overall health declined rapidly.

She decided that she would no longer be able to manage her personal affairs and had John appointed as her guardian. John's name was added to the home, which had been originally only in Susan's name, and was also added to all of her bank accounts, certificates of deposits, and other investments. The following year John became unable to care for himself and Susan, and both entered an assisted living facility. Shortly thereafter, John gave a power of attorney to his son, placing him in complete control of both spouses' funds. Within 5 days, the house had been quit-claim deeded to the son and the bank accounts fully depleted. A few weeks later John died.

When Susan's son telephoned the nursing home to speak with his mother, he was informed that she was unable to communicate. He then asked to speak with John and was informed that John had died. Shortly thereafter, Susan also died. When her children came to take care of the funeral arrangements and to settle her estate, they learned that there was nothing left. John's son had the power of attorney and was within his legal rights to dispose of all assets. None of the other family members received anything. Unfortunately for the families of Alice and Susan, the lesson learned has been a very costly one and is one that is learned across America.

It should be mentioned that limited powers of attorney, which set specific terms and the length of time an agent can use the document, are also available. Although having a limitation may appear to be more secure for the principal signing the document, a great amount of assets could disappear in a relatively short period of time. Consider the case of the wife who had a 90-day limited power of attorney from her husband. While he was incapacitated, she was able to sell their home, sell stocks and bonds, and have the proceeds placed only in her name and continue to cash his weekly disability paychecks that came through his employer's insurance coverage. By the time the 90 days were up and he was back on his feet, his wife was divorcing him, he no longer had any assets, and his whole life was in shambles.

In both of these cases, the powers of attorney had given the holders legal authority, and nothing could be done by law enforcement because no crime had been committed. The seniors' money was simply gone. However, this is not to say that the elderly should not ever consider a power of attorney. In fact, this may be their only option as they become more infirm or mentally unable to manage their affairs. Most of the time those who hold a power of attorney are truly interested in the welfare of the grantee and fulfill this power honestly and responsibly. It should also be mentioned that a power of attorney is only one of the many ways caregivers manage to help themselves to someone's money or possessions.

INVESTMENT SCAMS

Many elderly have accumulated comfortable sums of money for their retirement and need advice on investments. Family members may be too busy or too remote, or lack the knowledge necessary to handle the financial affairs of their parents or aged relatives. Therefore, professional help is sought with the result that investment advisors become financial caretakers of the elderly's funds and may take advantage of their senior clients.

Although in the 1990s the nation's violent crime rate decreased, financial crimes against the elderly increased as ever larger numbers of America's population moved into their golden years. In California, Santa Clara County developed the Financial Abuse Specialist Team (FAST) with a goal of providing a "rapid response to reports of financial abuse with an emphasis on the prevention of financial destitution." Up to the present time, FAST has prevented the loss of (or recovered total assets of) more than $71 million in real property, liquid assets, and stocks and bonds. In addition it has collected $2.5 million in restitution and recovery or settlement money.[5]

According to the AARP, low interest rates and an unpredictable stock market created a "perfect storm" for investment fraud against investors. Complex investment schemes such as promissory notes, charitable gift annuities, and Ponzi schemes (see Chapter 1) promise greatly inflated terms that are appealing to older persons who see their retirement funds dwindling.[6] Viatical settlements are another type of investment scheme. Originating as a way to help the gravely ill pay medical bills, they are interests in the death benefits (life insurance) of terminally ill patients. The North Carolina Division of Aging points out that, due to uncertainty predicting when someone will die, these investments are always risky and sometimes fraudulent.[7] However, for both young and old persons who are faced with rising living expenses or exist on fixed incomes, these scams are very appealing because they promise inflated returns on any investment.

Eighty-two-year-old retired Marine Colonel Ken Reusser of Oregon was promised a 36 percent return on his investment. Faced with some serious medical bills for his wife and on the advice of friends he met through a club called Life After 50, Reusser invested a considerable amount of his savings. He ended up losing $262,000, being forced into bankruptcy, and expecting to lose the mountain home he and his wife built. "I'm here as a very embarrassed individual," Reusser said at a news conference with state regulators, "We just trusted the people."[8]

Testifying before the Senate Subcommittee on Aging, Financial Abuse, and Exploitation, J. Joseph Curran, Jr., attorney general for the state of Maryland, cites numerous cases where members of investment firms cheated seniors who were purchasing financial advice. In one case an investment firm "borrowed" $350,000 from one client, an 89-year-old widow and retired schoolteacher. In another case a stockbroker churned an elderly couple's account so that it netted him more than $300,000 in commissions but caused them losses of a half million dollars. In both instances the Attorney General's office was able to get at least partial restitution.[9]

Another interesting example is that of Harry R. Krausman, a certified public accountant, who in 1995 was appointed conservator and co-guardian of Alberta Wittlich's estate. Krausman was arrested on October 6, 2003, and charged with theft and conspiracy for allegedly taking $1.9 million from Wittlich. Jo Ann Alford, Wittlich's niece, explained how her aunt had been able to amass a great deal of wealth and how Krausman had been able to embezzle a portion of Wittlich's funds simply because the family trusted him.

> I trusted him (Krausman) because we didn't have anyone else to trust. I should have kept closer track of him. But every time I talked to him, he said, "Everything is just fine," and he would send me papers. . . . I'm punishing myself . . . . She (Wittlich) told me she was the largest woman stockholder in US West. . . . My aunt had all tele-

communication stock. She never sold a single issue of stock. . . . She just kept buying.[10]

Apparently, the 100-year-old Wittlich trusted the accountant completely to manage her portfolio. After all, he was named as co-guardian, her investment caretaker, and it was expected that he would guard her funds. However, Krausman manipulated her investments, selling most of them and taking the rest of her money in the form of "loans" that went to various businesses in which Krausman, his family, or friends had an interest. Investigators indicated that a portion of the money was used by Krausman to "purchase the Lakewood Athletic Club, one of the largest clubs of its type in Denver's western suburbs."[11] Alford's lack of knowledge about investing or her inattention to her aunt's business arrangements resulted in tremendous loss of assets in the estate.

Civilians are not the only persons to be fleeced. Military retirees are also often targeted by untrustworthy caregivers. With a full disability retirement due to a head injury, Navy Commander Gloria Christensen needed help to manage her financial affairs. She asked for and was granted a custodian certified by the Department of Veterans Affairs. She learned that just by having access to an individual's social security number, irreparable damage can occur. While recuperating from her injury, Christensen received allotments from her tax-free disability payments, which were administered by her custodian. What she would learn later, to her dismay, was that the custodian was utilizing her social security number to "buy and sell stocks on the Internet"—racking up enough profits that the IRS came after her for more than $200,000 in back taxes.[12]

For many retired people like those in the above cases, investment advice can often result in catastrophic losses. This is not to imply, however, that most financial advisors or accountants are involved in fraud. Most are interested in taking excellent care of their client's investments and are incorruptible. Of course, there are always the exceptions, but these "financial fraudsters" are not the sleazy types one might imagine or that appear as stereotypes in the media. Many are highly trained professionals who have been very successful. They have not intentionally planned to harm their clients; however, they may find that siphoning money from customers' accounts is fairly easy, and the temptation to do so is simply too enticing. On the other hand, some who have control of an individual's portfolio may buy and sell that person's stock simply to get the commissions from the sales. The broker is not interested in the client's welfare or whether the client makes or loses money in the transactions; the chief goal is to increase the broker's income. Also, because stock transactions may generate a considerable amount of paper that is confusing to the average investor, the client may sign papers without fully understanding what the impact may be.

One investor paid $100,000 for what she *thought* was a federally insured certificate of deposit (CD). The financial advisor did use the investor's money to purchase the CDs, but he then used them as collateral for loans made out to him. He was able to do this because the investor had been induced to sign a contract naming the advisor as the trustee of the money. This permitted him to cash the CDs and spend the money as he wished.[13] In this instance, her giving up control of her finances was the problem, and her trust that her financial advisor would look out for her interest was sadly misplaced.

THE NURSING HOME

As they age, individuals usually need not only financial advice but some type of physical care. Most elderly persons will, at one time or another, have to live for an extended period of time in an assisted living or a nursing facility—that place between home and death. A broken hip, a debilitating illness, or the requirement for extended physical therapy may make this necessary. In fact, it's estimated that nearly 1.5 million elderly or disabled are in nursing homes at the present time and receive more than $58 billion a year from state and federal health insurance plans.[14] Although children or relatives may wish to be available on a daily basis to ensure that proper care and attention is being given to the patient, this is usually not feasible. Therefore, problems may arise, not just in regard to possible physical abuse, but regarding their loved one's money or possessions.

Judy Ann Williamson, who worked as an office manager, embezzled a total of $672,240 from the Mountain View Care Center and Life Care Centers of America. In her Life Care position, the enormous amount she was able to steal included $21,000 from checks sent by relatives to the home's residents. Apparently, Williamson took charge of the checks, endorsed them to herself, and deposited them in her bank account. The homes have had to reimburse the patient's accounts, and Mountain View has reimbursed Medicaid. Both institutions hope to be able to recover some of their losses from their former employee. It was found that Williamson (who was convicted on two felony counts) spent $200,000 of the stolen money to purchase various kinds of perfume, but so far officials have not been able to locate the other $400,000.[15] In this instance the elderly residents were lucky enough to have their funds returned.

Carol Scott, President of the National Association of Long Term Care Ombudsman, testifying at a Senate hearing on financial exploitation of the elderly, related numerous instances of nursing home fraud in Missouri. Mary, a 91-year-old, had been taken by an individual, who had her power of attorney, to visit someone at a home and simply left there. She had signed the document while hospitalized and could not remember having done so. However, utilizing the power and without Mary's knowledge or consent, the holder sold one of her farms and many of her household items. In another case, an aide at a Missouri nursing home stole large sums of money from three of the residents. In yet another case, a home resident was persuaded to put her niece's name on a bank account. This was a grave mistake because the niece then purchased furniture, jewelry, and clothes and made payments on a new house with her aunt's money. The theft of over $60,000 was discovered when a pharmacy refused to send the elderly woman's medication because of past-due bills.[16] (Fortunately, some restitution was made in all of these cases.)

In Colorado an elderly woman who was confined to a nursing home to recover from surgery asked her sister to bring $6,000 to the facility because she wanted to order some new furniture for her return to her own home. The sister did as she was asked, and shortly thereafter the police report in the local newspaper indicated that all but a few hundred dollars was missing from the drawer where it had been placed. The patient reported that someone at the nursing facility had taken the money but this could not be proved. When the sister was questioned about why she would take $6,000 to the home, she replied, "Well, she told me to get the money for her. I just did what I was told to do."

This unfortunate scenario occurs frequently, usually with disastrous results. Although people are warned not to keep large sums of money with them when they are patients in hospitals or recovering in nursing homes, they continue to do so. Most hospitals ask that all valuables, including money, be listed at the time of admittance and encourage patients to have family or friends take the valuables out of the institution. Almost all facilities do not have places for safekeeping of valuables.

Of course, valuables include many items other than money. Credit cards, PIN numbers, or jewelry of all kinds should not be left in care centers open to the public. These items can be invitations for theft by unscrupulous employees. A woman who worked for several years at a nursing home explained what frequently happened.

> Shirley came to the home after falling and breaking her hip and ankle. She was not mobile for several weeks and was also on some pain medication, so she was not always aware of her surroundings. In fact, she slept a great deal of the time. During the first weeks, her engagement ring simply disappeared. I'm not sure she was even aware that it was missing. It was her daughter who questioned where it had been placed. It was just gone. Someone had taken it, and, as I recall it was a little over a half carat diamond. The family was quite upset about the incident, but nothing could be done. Employee turnover is rapid in these type of environments, and any one of a dozen people could have removed the ring from her finger. I guess I wonder why her wedding band was not stolen also.

Another problem with patients, whether male or female, is the theft of clothing. Many times families bring robes, pajamas, and gowns for their family member. Sometimes friends send or bring these items as gifts, and many are new. "My father-in-law was in a nursing home for about 3 months," one woman stated, "and the help was always commenting about how nice his clothes were. They weren't anything special, just some pretty cardigans and wash slacks, but when he died, they were simply gone." She went on to explain that the family would have given the clothing to the

Salvation Army and didn't care particularly about the missing items, "but it just shows that things are not always returned to the family. Suppose it had been jewelry or a good watch."

Another woman mentioned the fact that her mother's gowns and robes repeatedly disappeared while the woman was convalescing from hip replacement surgery.

> My mother took several very nice nightgowns and a beautiful Adonna quilted robe with her to the home; the robe disappeared almost immediately. I replaced it with another pretty pink Vanity Fair matching robe and gown. Those items cost around $45 and within 2 weeks were gone. I bought a third set, took a letter to the director of the facility and had him initial that the clothes were on the premises. The letter stated that I would hold the home responsible if any more of my mother's clothing went missing. Apparently that did the trick for we had no more problems.

Caregivers do not just defraud their charges; sometimes the fraud involves American taxpayers as well. Janet Reno named health care fraud the Department of Justice's number two priority, second only to violent crime, and the Clinton administration declared war on regulating health care fraud and abuse.[17] Cases of health care fraud involving the aged are found wherever these people receive services.

Take the case of Pauline Moskal whose mother Agnes Bogan was suffering from Parkinson's disease and was in Fairhaven nursing home southwest of Chicago. Although Pauline did not believe this to be a terminal illness, a representative of Samaritan Care (a not-for-profit hospice established in 1992 by Joseph A. Kirschenbaum) convinced her that Agnes would benefit from hospice care. Pauline was not certain her mother qualified for the hospice service but had watched other patients at the home receive more attention from the staff than her mother was getting. When she questioned a person from the hospice regarding her mother's eligibility, she was told, "It's a government program and the money is just sitting there and you may as well do it."[18] Because Pauline wanted the best care possible for her mother, she agreed to the recommendation from the Samaritan Care representative.

The primary requirement for hospice care is that the patient have 6 months or less to live. As this specialized care for people on the brink of death has boomed, so has fraud and abuse in nursing homes, hospices and assisted-care centers designed to serve the nation's growing aging population. Sometimes doctors do not even visit potential hospice patients but still certify that the service is needed. Agnes Bogan, who had been certified by Samaritan's doctor as terminally ill, remained in the program for 7 months before she was removed under unclear circumstances. She finally did die nearly 16 months later from pneumonia—not Parkinson's disease.[19] Still, because the exact date of death cannot be predicted, the claim can be made that Bogan's illness did not progress as had been anticipated, and, as with many cases, little can be done to prove any fraud was intended.

At several other nursing home facilities, routine eye exams were offered free to all patients. Although Medicare did not cover these exams, the nursing staff provided patient information to the optometry practice performing the exams. The optometrists, in turn, used this information as the basis for billing Medicare. True, the nursing home patients did receive free eye exams, but Medicare was billed for several other optometry services that were never provided.[20]

Between 1993 and 1996, a Toledo, Ohio, firm sold incontinence kits (adult diapers) to nursing homes, billing them to Medicare as "female urinary collection devices" and charging between $8.34 and $22.57. The firm had originally purchased the diapers for between 25 and 45 cents. William Harris, owner of the firm, eventually pleaded guilty to a count of conspiring to submit $42 million in false claims to Medicare and of laundering $9 million.[21]

CAREGIVERS FOR HIRE

Of course, many elderly individuals refuse to go to a nursing home or do not have the necessary money or insurance to cover the large monthly charges. Those children living long distances from their extended family will face the necessity of hiring a stranger to come daily into the home and tend to their elderly parents. This gives the in-home caregiver unlimited opportunities to take advantage of those left in their care.

Often this companion, nurse, or housekeeper can gain knowledge about an elder's checking or savings account merely by offering to write checks for the account owner to sign and thus help with the burden of paying monthly bills. Sometimes, however, the older person can be tricked into signing blank checks, as was the case with 89-year-old John, who resided in Amarillo but who was visited fairly often by his son Mark, an engineer living in Dallas.

We didn't live close to Dad, but we drove up to Amarillo at least once every 2 months. Dad was retired from his own successful business and wasn't senile. He was still fairly active in the community, but after mom died, he had hired a housekeeper and cook of sorts who came in 3 days a week. She had shown references and actually kept things around the house in pretty good shape. However, Dad didn't like shopping for household items or for groceries, so he would merely give Maria a signed check when she went to the store. Also, he never took time to check what the money was being spent for. Mom had always taken care of the household expenses, and he had no idea what food cost or whether new towels were needed.

At any rate, he just happened to mention once that it cost a great deal to run a household and that he had never before realized just how much. I was puzzled by this comment and asked to look through his bank statements. The check for his groceries each week was running over $200, and he ate out a great deal with golfing friends. When I asked to see the checkout slips for the groceries, he admitted that he had never asked Maria for them.

I stayed a few days with Dad, and when Maria next went to the store with his signed check, I asked to see the itemized checkout slip. At first, Maria said she must have dropped it when loading the grocery bags in her car. However, a little prodding produced the slip. On it were many items not used by dad and which she was purchasing for her own family. Also, there was a $50 cash back item listed. Maria could not explain the reason for getting the money, got very huffy, left, and never came back.

I had the store manager talk with his checkout clerks, and they stated that Maria received money every time she bought groceries, which was usually twice a week. I talked with the police about arresting Maria, but it was going to be difficult to actually prove that she had taken money from Dad as she had been smart enough to destroy all grocery sales slips. We never did know how much money was missing, but I'm certain it would have been several thousand dollars. We didn't call the police as Dad really liked Maria and didn't want to get her in trouble. So, we got another housekeeper, and Maria moved on. I imagine she is probably housekeeping for another elderly person and probably ripping them off, too.

A similar case occurred in Detroit where a 31-year-old woman acquired access to an 81-year-old's checking account. The young woman had been a longtime acquaintance and was helping the oldster with household chores and shopping and was finally requested to aid in paying monthly bills. Over the next 2 years, without the elderly lady's knowledge, the helper withdrew enough money from the account to purchase a sports car, an air conditioning unit, and to remodel her home. Eventually the victim realized what had happened when she went to the bank to withdraw some money and found that the account had been almost fully depleted. She did report the crime to the police; however, Sterling Heights (Michigan) Detective Edward King, who has handled many cases of fraud against seniors, indicated that arresting the thief and ordering her to pay back the stolen money would be useless. "It would be trying to get blood from a turnip," he said.[22] Law enforcement officials point out that restitution is very difficult to achieve in most of these cases.

Although many elderly are careful about signing blank checks, relatives or caregivers often have access to these checkbooks and forge the signatures. After all, banks cannot economically employ enough people to check the signatures on the thousands of checks that are received daily, and the signatures of many individual may be almost a scribble and nearly illegible. The check is paid by the bank based on the account number printed at the bottom, making it easy for someone to obtain funds falsely.

One family with a 74-year-old paralyzed father obtained from their local senior citizens center the name of what they thought was a reputable health care agency. The agency provided them with a young woman from Georgia in the former Soviet Union to assist the invalid. The woman explained that she did not have a social security number yet since she was new to the United States and asked for her weekly salary of $520 to be paid in cash. The family became suspicious as the weeks went by without the woman getting the social security card; however, the father said he was getting good care and would not hear of her being dismissed. Later the family discovered that their father and the woman (who was an illegal alien and not authorized to work in the United States) had been secretly married for 17 months.[23] In this way she avoided deportation and, eventually, got control of her elderly husband's assets.

Another source of easy money for the unscrupulous person is credit cards that are often entrusted to the caregiver and used fraudulently for the caregiver's needs, leaving the elderly victim without funds or owing horrendous credit card charges. Also, large numbers of credit cards can be obtained from a victim without that person's knowledge because most homes are inundated with letters offering these handy bits of plastic. Filling out the application form or a quick call to the credit card company usually results in credit being extended. If someone other than the authorized holder is using the card, it may be several months before the theft is discovered. In addition, the blank checks that are included with many credit card offers often tempt caregivers to forge a signature and take money from their charges' accounts.

For those wishing to steal from the elderly, ATMs are another source of easy money. Many senior citizens have trouble remembering their PIN numbers; therefore, they have the tendency to keep them attached to their ATM cards. This makes the PIN numbers readily accessible to any caregiver wishing to deplete a person's account quickly without having to forge any document. The only time law enforcement could catch a culprit would be by utilizing photos from the video cameras at the ATM; however, the tapes must be viewed almost immediately after the crime because the camera tapes usually are kept only a short period of time.

Sometimes caregivers will deny relatives access to their elderly charge. If this happens, something may be amiss, as was the case with Audrey Smith's aunt. When Audrey would telephone her 80-year-old aunt, the woman's caregivers would say that she was too tired to talk on the phone or was sleeping. Eventually, Smith stopped calling and did not learn that her aunt, the granddaughter of a former Kansas governor, was the victim of a scam until state officials called her. Smith was to learn that the caregivers had cleaned out the aunt's bank account of several hundred thousand dollars, coerced her to change her will, and sold all of her possessions. Smith, who lives in Texas, said that she felt "so guilty about not pushing the issue."[24] Of course, without going to visit or insisting that the aunt speak to her, there was little Smith could have done. Her aunt simply was made unavailable to her repeated calls.

Krystal Puccetti, a 39-year-old caregiver for several senior citizens, was able to profit to the tune of $97,000 in just the year 2000. Going to a credit union with an 85-year-old client, she was able to open three loan accounts totaling $31,122. "Authorities also found several credit card accounts, one with an $11,000 balance, had been opened in the member's account without her knowledge [and] with the caretaker as the authorized user."[25] This was not her only conquest, as Puccetti was also being investigated on allegations of bilking another one of her elderly patients.

In addition to nonfamily caregivers, adult children who are forced to oversee the care of elderly parents or other relatives may begin to dip into their charge's funds. Usually the children have made some sacrifice in time away from their own families or time away from their careers or jobs. They may, then, feel entitled to dip into mom's or uncle's money. After all, they rationalize, they should be paid for the cleaning or grocery shopping they do. If they are continually carting the elderly persons to and from doctor's offices, shouldn't they be reimbursed for the gasoline used in their cars or for new tires? Eventually, the elderly person's assets are being used to help support the children's lifestyle.

After one elderly man's wife had died, his daughter kept coming into the family home and appropriating various household items. "It was a pot here, some towels there," he stated. "I don't think she came to see how I was doing; she needed something and didn't have the money to buy it. She was always a spendthrift. Finally, I told her to stop taking things out of the house. I made it pretty clear, 'Your mother's dead, but as you can see, *I'm not dead yet!*'" He concluded by mentioning that the daughter seldom visited him after his comment.

One young man bilked his grandmother out of $131,000, which forced her into bankruptcy and forced her to return to work at age 70. She had used up her life savings and had taken cash advances on her credit cards to provide him with the money. When his grandmother eventually reported him to the police, the grandson admitted to police that he had been "deceitful and untruthful" when he told the woman he needed the money for child-support payments, bank fees, electricity bills, and rent. However, he further stated that he didn't look at his actions as stealing.[26] She had given him the money. He finally stopped asking his grandmother for money when he realized that she didn't have any more to give him. The fact that the aging woman was back in the labor force merely to support herself didn't bother the grandson at all.

Sometimes, as in the case of Phyllis L., caregivers not only steal but also abuse their elderly charges. Phyllis suffered from the early stages of Alzheimer's disease and could not be left alone in her home. Her daughter, who lived over a hundred miles away, hired a live-in caretaker because her mother was fearful of being placed in assisted living or a nursing facility.

About a month after the caretaker had been on the job, the daughter came to visit. When she arrived, she found her mother alone and locked in the bathroom. She also discovered that many of her mother's antiques were not in their usual spots. The caregiver did not return to the home for nearly 5 hours. Upon questioning her, the woman said, "I had errands to run and didn't trust your mother because she tends to wander off. I locked her in the bathroom so that she would have the facilities." When asked where the antiques had been stored, the caretaker replied that the mother had given those items to her and that she had sold them. The daughter fired the caretaker but was unable to press charges. Because the mother was lucid some of the time, she could have given the items away, thus not making it theft.

CAUTION PAYS

Although preventing caretaker fraud is difficult, families with elderly relatives can take a number of actions that may be of help. Hiring caretakers through a reputable employment agency and insuring that the caretakers are experienced, bonded, and have references is essential. Too many families rely on word-of-mouth references or, due to time requirements, take anyone who is interested in the job. Visiting or telephoning the elderly more often keeps family members in touch with the senior's needs and also gives them some indication of the relationship between the senior and the caretaker. Try and become aware if a romantic relationship is developing with a very young individual and the senior citizen because this is not the normal type of romantic entanglement. Getting the elderly person to set up bank accounts which require two signatures (the senior and a family member) makes it more difficult for con artists to strip a bank account. Making inquiries about the senior's investment advisors may forestall possible loss of badly needed retirement funds.

Also (as the editors of CNN and *Money* magazine indicate), there are some warning signs, both financial and in the demeanor of the elderly individual, that should alert family members to the swindles.

- Caretaker is secretive or evasive when you ask about your relative.
- Caretaker seems to be keeping the relative from other loved ones.
- Household or personal items are missing.
- Changes in personal hygiene or wearing worn or inappropriate clothing.
- A spate of new acquaintances who may be accomplices of the hired companion.
- Numerous unpaid bills, such as overdue utilities, taxes, mortgage payment.
- Elderly person fearful or seems afraid to speak in front of caregiver.
- Caregiver leaves without giving notice and is untraceable.
- A power of attorney has been drawn up without family knowledge.
- Sudden changes in a senior's will.
- Changes in names on savings and checking accounts.
- Recent changes to title of home in favor of a caring "friend."
- Caregiver evasive about financial arrangements for his or her companionship.
- Elderly and companion give conflicting accounts of an incident, expenditure, or financial need.

- Senior complains that he or she used to have money, but does not have it anymore.
- Senior is fearful that he or she will outlive their finances even though the individual may be known to be financially well off.
- ATM withdrawals when the senior cannot walk or get to the bank.
- Credit cards taken out by the senior with companion's name added to the card.

It must be remembered that some elderly may be mentally impaired and may not be able to realize fraud has occurred, to report victimization, or to describe the details. Many times, if the individual is mentally incompetent, authorities and family may tend to discredit the report of financial mismanagement. If the victims are in a nursing facility, isolated from family and friends, and totally dependent on the hired staff, they may be fearful of reporting problems for fear of retaliation. In addition, if the perpetrator is a family member, many elderly simply do not want to accuse relatives because this may cause them trouble with the law or destroy the solidarity of the family. Therefore, those who truly care about senior family members and who wish to prevent possible fraud must be alert and must find the time to help oversee the physical, mental, and financial well being of their loved ones.

Chapter Seven

Looking for Love

---

ools? Or just lonely and, as the poems and songs warn, searching for love and finding heartache instead. When an elderly person loses a spouse or close companion, it is often difficult to find other companionship. Adult children are busy with their careers and their own families and have little time to spend with their lonely and grieving parent. The individuals who now find themselves again single often seek to assuage their loneliness by joining community groups, participating in local senior recreational activities, or getting on the Internet. For unsuspecting individuals, that charming lady or gentleman they meet may not be simply another lonely person looking for love but, instead, may be merely in search of a lonely victim who can provide money or other assets. These scams go under various headings—Romeo Rip-Off, Cyber-Romeo, and Sweetheart Swindle. Although individuals can be fleeced by romantic entanglements, nothing illegal may have occurred. These relationships are entered into on a voluntary basis. Proving that individuals were victims of sweetheart swindles can be difficult if, for example, they willingly gave money to someone "because of love."

There may be more elderly female victims of romance simply because women tend to outlive men. This means that there are not enough elderly men to meet the demand of females who no longer have a spouse or male friend. Statistics show that approximately 74 percent of men over age 65 live with a spouse but only 40 percent of women do. Forty-one percent of women over age 65 live alone, many of them widows, but just 16 percent of men do.[1] Although some elderly who have lost spouses are able to remarry, for women widowhood is usually a permanent status. This makes them particularly vulnerable to conniving Romeos who haunt church groups, social clubs, and other venues where widows (especially well-off widows) congregate.

Those who have spent most of their lives as one part of a couple find themselves suddenly classified as single. Singles, whether widowed or divorced, are then forced to rearrange their lives. Although some compensate for their loss by talking with relatives or friends, many do not have close confidants or family living nearby. Those older and divorced are more likely to be living alone and more likely to feel lonely without someone to discuss or share things.[2] Many older singles also are likely to feel lonely due to low income that limits their social contacts or due to ill health and depression. Used to having a companion for shopping, dining, and travel, women tend to become isolated from society, adding to their lonely feelings.

Seeking companionship to alleviate this loneliness, women often become victims of the Romeo Rip-Off, in which a bored, lonely, or lovelorn target is wooed by a professed lover. As women get drawn into what they hope will be long-term, rewarding relationships, their lovers are steadily depleting their bank accounts or other assets. Seventy-one-year-old Augusta "Augie" K. learned a hard lesson about friendship and fraud as she lost at least $30,000 to the man to whom "she had already lost her heart."[3]

Once Dan was gone, I was so alone. I guess I didn't realize until then how much I was used to his taking me places and usually being with me, especially when he retired. My son lived a thousand miles away so I only saw him and his family at the holidays. For a while, couples Dan and I had known would invite me to go places with them, but I soon found myself sort of like extra or unwanted baggage. So I began either staying home or going to a movie or out to eat by myself. It was not enjoyable, and I really missed having someone to do things with.

Then, at a church reception, I met Howard who had recently moved to town. He was nice looking; in fact, he was quite handsome for his age. Although he was 5 years younger than me and could have dated a much younger woman, he seemed to be attracted to me and was very attentive. Not pushy, you understand, just very considerate, very caring. I was so flattered by the attention, so glad to have an escort.

After just a few weeks, Howard asked me to marry him, and we decided to have a ceremony a few months later and then take a trip to Hawaii for our honeymoon. He mentioned that, since we were now engaged, it might make sense for him to move into my home. After all, he was renting an apartment and could save money for the honeymoon by doing this. At first I was a little bit hesitant as I wondered what my friends would say, but after all, society now views things like this differently, so I finally agreed. Soon his clothes were in the closet and his car was in the garage.

About a week after Howard moved in, he explained that he had gotten a letter from his financial advisor, and there was a problem with some of his investments—some from overseas, which had been tied up for some reason—and he hadn't gotten a deposit which usually came automatically to his checking account. He said that he needed some quick cash as he didn't want any short checks on his bank account. I loaned him $3,000 because he said it would only be a short time loan of a few weeks. A few days later, I received a telephone call from a man who claimed to be Howard's financial advisor and who asked to speak with him. When I said Howard wasn't home, the man asked who I was. When I said that Howard and I were engaged, he explained to me that Howard needed to send him immediately $15,000 to "clinch a deal" for some stock he wanted to purchase. The man said if the money didn't arrive by the next day, Howard would lose out on the deal. He emphasized that there was a great deal of money to be made on the deal.

When Howard returned, I explained the situation as best I could; however, Howard reminded me that he couldn't get at some of his funds, which were still tied up overseas. He seemed very depressed that he couldn't take advantage of the good stock deal, so, foolishly I now realize, I loaned him the required $15,000 plus the commission fee of $1,500. Two days later Howard disappeared.

At first, I called the police and reported that he was a missing person as though something terrible had happened to him. Now I know that he merely skipped out on me. The police found that his name wasn't Howard, that he was only 58 years old, and that he owed rent for the apartment he had been living in before he moved into my home. They were also able to learn that someone fitting his description had charmed an elderly woman in Ohio into thinking he would marry her and had gotten over $40,000 before moving on. There may have been other women who had been taken in, but the police could trace him no further.

"What fools both this other woman in Ohio and I were," Augie said, slowly shaking her head in disgust at being so gullible. "I just can't believe I was so stupid, so needy of having someone around to keep me company. And I can't believe there are people out there who would do something so mean and hurtful to another human being. Believe me, from now on I won't trust anyone. I just don't know how it is possible these days to meet someone nice."[4]

THE TEMPTING ADVERTISEMENT

For many seeking a nice companion, it is an advertisement on the Internet, in a magazine, or in a newspaper that leads to their locating that special someone and, often, to their downfall. *W/Male, 64, fun-loving with good sense of humor, seeking w/female same or close age for day trips, movies, dining. Box X23.* Although this sounds almost too good to be true, it also sounds very enticing to the unwary.

This type of advertisement can be found in the classified section and sometimes on a special page of many newspapers across the country. It beckons to all of the women seeking to find companionship in their declining years. Many of these ads are simply honest calls from one lonely person to other lonely persons. However, some are scams aimed at those eager to establish new relationships, which can lure the unwary into both financial loss and loss of self-esteem, as 69-year-old Maryann R. discovered.

After some pushing and prodding by friends, I became brave enough to answer an ad in my local newspaper and began corresponding with Brad, who was my age and who lived in a neighboring state. We wrote back and forth for several months. I was in good health, didn't feel nor look my age, and hadn't had much attention since my husband died several years ago. Brad was charming and witty in his letters; we exchanged photos, and he was very complimentary about mine. I needed his compliments. It was great to talk to my other women friends and to tell them what Brad had written and to show them the small gifts he sent. His letters became more amorous and so did mine. To put it mildly, I was in love.

When Brad suggested that he come and visit me for a while so that we could get better acquainted and maybe make plans for the future, I was delighted. My home, the one my husband and I had owned, was a very nice one with plenty of room, and I got everything ready for Brad's visit—bragging to my friends that I felt he was coming out to propose. Brad arrived, and he was like his photos, tall, trim, with a shock of graying hair. For his age he was really quite good-looking. I was the envy of all my friends, particularly the other ones who, like me, were widowed or those who were divorced.

A few weeks went by, and Brad and I went all sorts of places, were also invited to my friends' homes and just, generally, enjoyed ourselves. We had not become intimate during this time, and Brad always acted the perfect gentleman. However, as the few weeks' visit turned into a few months and nothing had been said about a permanent relationship, I began to wonder if I had taken too much for granted in Brad's letters. Also, I noticed that I was the one generally picking up the tab when we ate out or went to a movie. Brad explained that he had lost some traveler's checks and was waiting for them to be reissued. But the checks never turned up. When I finally asked about them, he had an explanation for that, too. He said that they must have been sent to his home address even though he had notified the company that he would be with me. He had arrived by plane, so he had to use my car, and he began taking it on trips by himself—making the excuse that he was visiting a cousin or attending to some financial matters. He said that he had a lot of stock to look after—an extensive portfolio was the way he put it—that he had to manage and watch over carefully.

I believed all of this because I wanted to believe it. None of it was true. Finally, after his sponging off of me for 5 months, I confronted him about our relationship. Naturally, there *was no relationship!* I was just an easy mark for him to get free board and room. I found out later that he wasn't even in his sixties; he was only 56 and made his livelihood by writing to lonely women who answered his "lonely hearts" ad. I knew he received mail at my home but always thought it was business mail. Actually, as I discovered after I threw him out, it was mail from other women whom he was "setting up." I felt like such a fool. There was nothing I could do. Technically he hadn't committed any crime. I had invited him to visit, and I had been stupid enough to finance his living expenses. My friends were sympathetic to my face, but I'll bet I was the target of much laughter behind my back. I was so ashamed that I almost stopped returning phone calls or seeing anyone.

For Bonnie M., another victim looking for love, romance showed up at her place of employment. At age 69 Bonnie was still working part-time as a beautician when an extremely good-looking older man came in to get his hair cut and styled. During the course of the haircut, the two chatted about a number of things, and before he left he told her his name was Don and asked her to dinner that night. Although Bonnie was hesitant at first, she finally decided she would meet Don at a local restaurant. After all, she would drive herself and could leave whenever she chose.

She recalled that they "had a lovely dinner, with wine, and he brought me a nosegay of violets. I was so pleased by all of the attention." Then, that same night, Don proposed! Bonnie laughed and demurred, not taking him seriously. Still, she was flattered by his interest and said, "The thought that I might start a new life again was hard to believe. It made me feel so young, so giddy and pleased."

Over the next few weeks, Don courted Bonnie and persisted with his proposals of marriage; finally Bonnie accepted. The pair went to a local jeweler where Don insisted that Bonnie select a $3,000 engagement ring so she could "show her friends how much he loved her." Bonnie never questioned the cost of the ring or if he had the financial means to pay for it as she was "just in seventh heaven."

Shortly thereafter, Don invited Bonnie on a trip to Albuquerque and encouraged her to go with him to look at motor homes. Further, he told her that he had four cars and persuaded her to get rid of her automobile. He also encouraged her to contact a real estate agent in order to sell her house because they would need to purchase a new home after they were married. Bonnie also noticed that in the couple of months they had been together Don had become very possessive, wanting to know who she had seen or who she was talking to on the telephone and not wanting her out of his sight except when she was working. What saved Bonnie from misfortune was simply a chance meeting with another woman.

I had a former boyfriend who was in trouble and who needed me to go to court with him to testify about where he had been on a particular evening several months before I met Don. While I was waiting to be called into the courtroom, I met a woman named Rita and we struck up a conversation. She told me she was dating a guy who she expected to marry. She showed me a photo of her intended, and guess what? It was Don.

When I said as much, she didn't believe me. But we began comparing notes. Sure enough. He was telling her the same lies he told me and was getting money from her also. In fact, she had quite a bit of his clothing and other gear at her apartment. That was where he went when I was at work.

As soon as I could get out of the court, I called Don and asked him if he were seeing any other women except me. He became very upset and said I was foolish to even think such a thing. However, when I told him I had some of his things, which I had picked up at Rita's apartment, he knew the game was up. By the time I got to my house, he was gone, and I never saw nor heard of him again—not that I wanted to!

Bonnie had a stroke of luck in that she found out about the scam in time, before she sold her home and, possibly, married Don. Some lonely women, however, are not that lucky and fall for schemes so ludicrous that it is difficult to believe they could be so naive or to sympathize with the victim. A classic example is that of Agnes D., age 62.

Dining alone at a restaurant, Agnes was picked up by Arnold, or Arnie as he liked to be called, who was dressed in shorts, a Hawaiian print shirt, and thongs. Agnes discovered that he was living nearby at a seedy motel, but he explained that he had a money order for 2 million dollars coming from overseas. Dressed only in the shorts and thongs, he also was able to convince a local bank that the money would arrive shortly, and, unbelievably, he was allowed to open a checking account based on the elusive funds.

Arnie wined and dined Agnes but always on her credit cards, which he said he would pay when his money arrived, and he gave her a check to show his good faith. He also bought her some lovely, very expensive gifts, always giving the stores a check and asking them to hold the check until his funds arrived. If they had called the bank to verify if he had funds, they would have gotten the same story—the money will be coming shortly from overseas. The check would eventually be honored. Arnie was even able to put $75,000 as down payment on a house, again asking the mortgage company to hold the check. The company also followed his wishes.

As the romance between Arnie and Agnes progressed, he invited her to California to see his home there. Upon reaching the airport, he told her that he had forgotten the plane tickets, so Agnes dutifully shelled out her credit card for the purchase, and the two boarded the plane, with Arnie still in his usual garb—shorts, shirt, and thongs. When they arrived in Los Angeles, Arnie rented a car (on Agnes' credit card) and drove her to a beautiful home—a mansion, in fact. This was his house, he told her. However, he explained that there was a problem with his getting into the home as it was in the process of major remodeling, so she couldn't have a tour of the premises at that time.

Finally, after about a month, Arnie disappeared, leaving Agnes, the bank, several merchants, a realtor, and a mortgage company holding worthless checks. When Agnes went to the motel to look for Arnie, she was told that he had registered with only a small duffle bag and had left without checking out and paying his bill. By then Agnes was out several thousand dollars that she had let Arnie put on her credit card. The interesting thing here is not just the willingness of those involved to go along with Arnie or Arnie's ability to pull the wool over so many eyes. It is the fact that because people agreed to hold the checks, they had entered into a civil contract. Therefore, Arnie (if he could have been located) could not have been charged with writing bad checks. Hopefully, out of all of this, Agnes learned not to be too trusting—and to be suspicious of charming men whose only clothing seem to be shorts, shirt, and thongs!

Of course, elderly men can also become victims of love. Those males who have lost a spouse are many times left with feelings of helplessness, particularly with regard to daily household chores such as cooking, house cleaning, laundry, ironing, and so forth. Many hurriedly seek remarriage or at least a companion for cohabitation. Although most of these arrangements are genuinely satisfying, some of the men end up without their money or their "honey."

This certainly was the case for Bob Lund of Citrus Heights, California, who feels he was the victim of Gypsy scam artists who practice romantic fraud instead of repair fraud. Having lunch in a fast-food restaurant, Lund was approached by Kisie Peaches Tina

John, age 25, who began to flirt with him. The relationship developed and the 73-year-old fell in love with her and wished to please her. First, he withdrew $100,000 in cash from his bank and gave it to her; then, he bought a new $36,000 pickup, on credit, for Kisie and other members of her family circle. Still unaware or unwilling to believe that he was merely the mark in her scam, he tried to buy a $65,000 Corvette for her, but at the last minute the auto salesman became suspicious and notified the California Highway Patrol. When Kisie was eventually arrested (and pled guilty to abetting a swindle), did Lund press for prosecution? No! He pleaded that she should be let out on bail until her trial, and posted the bail. Kisie repaid his kindness by skipping bail and leaving the area. Finally Lund was forced to admit "She's no good."[5] When examples such as this turn up—and they are fairly frequent—one wonders how so many people are willing and able to take advantage of another's good nature and trust. One might also wonder how a man of such advanced years and experience could so easily believe that such a young woman would instantly be attracted to him.

Recently, case histories regarding Gypsy romance scams have been receiving publicity on the Internet. In an article entitled "My Father's Journals," Candice Dobelstein Botner shows her father's involvement with an Annie M. Eventually the two "were married Gypsy style." While the Gypsies partied in another part of the hall, he was made to sit in another room by himself and given only a hard-boiled egg for his wedding dinner. Apparently, Botner's father financed Annie and her family, who exploited the elderly man's generosity to the tune of over $300,000.[6]

Another Web site commenting on the Gypsies and sweetheart scams cites an organized crime unit from the Phoenix Police Department. It indicates that, although victims can be found anywhere, the most popular contact points are grocery stores, banks, and casinos. Usually the elderly man is craving attention, and this is what the young woman provides. After a period of time after their friendship has blossomed, she will have some problems with which she needs financial help. The victim usually will lend her money to help out, and she promises to pay the loan back. Then may come the story that she needs to get a job but has no car. Can she borrow his or will he help her purchase one? She may eventually tell the victim that she loves him and promise marriage. Then she may ask that he make her beneficiary of his will or insurance policies.[7]

Usually marriage does not occur unless there is some type of property involved. If it is real estate, a transfer to a joint tenancy deed allows the Gypsy bride (upon her husband's death) to gain sole control of the property without having to go through probate. Even with a marriage, many times the new wife only stays in her husband's home infrequently. Problems within her family are the excuse used most often.[8] Generally, once the elderly husband has been bilked of all of his assets, he is simply abandoned, and the bride moves on to a new conquest. The befuddled husband may not realize for several days that his bride is gone until he realizes his financial security has gone with her.

Of course, those other than Gypsies are often quick to take the opportunity for romance to lead them to wealth. The distraught daughter of an 81-year-old man explained that her father had become the victim of an old and well-loved family friend, Yvonne.

> Yvonne had been around our family for years, and was considered to be almost like one of the family. She had already married and buried two husbands, so after my mother died, she was around the house a great deal to help out. All of us were very appreciative.
>
> My dad was inconsolable until about 3 months ago. Suddenly, he perked up considerably and really became a "horny" little old man. He began calling women he and mom had known, those who were now widows, and said he wanted to marry again. He approached a couple of my friends and asked them to move in with him, even though they were my age. I was so embarrassed for him and me, too.
>
> Then, he told me he had called Yvonne and within just a couple of days she had moved into the house. Almost immediately, she discouraged me and my brothers and sisters from calling Dad; she changed the locks on all of the doors and kept the house locked most of the time. We had to make an appointment to see our father. Occasionally, we were able to talk to Dad when she was out of the house, and he mentioned things he has bought for her kids. Well, actually, they aren't kids; they're my age.
>
> Yvonne has talked him into selling property that was from my mom's side of the family. My mother always wanted that property to be split among me and my brothers and sisters. Now it's gone. The few times I tried to talk with Dad about Yvonne, he just got angry and shut me out even further. If I really thought she loved

him, I guess I wouldn't be so angry myself. But, I think his savings are all gone, and they're living just on his pension check. Dad wasn't wealthy, but he did have quite a bit in savings and other investments. Also, over the few months they've been together—I don't know if they really got married—his physical appearance has changed. The few times I've seen him, he looks dirty and unkempt, and the house is not tidy. I think Yvonne's merely going to clean out all of his assets, and when the money's all gone, she will be, too.

The daughter and her siblings contacted a lawyer but were advised that there was nothing to be done. The father had not been declared incompetent to handle his affairs, and, apparently, he was a willing participant in the household arrangements.

Since elderly men are in short supply, if they are fairly healthy (and fairly comfortable financially, like the case above), there are usually a bevy of single women from which to choose for marriage or just companionship. Some of these females will be looking for largesse rather than love as another 79-year-old man related in an interview.

After my wife had been dead for several months, I decided I needed to get my life going again. So I joined the Eagles Lodge and began regularly attending some of the dances. I still could "cut a rug" pretty well, still had hair and my own teeth, and was popular with the ladies. Well, let's just admit it. I was one of the few men there who was still pretty physically and mentally fit.

At any rate, eventually I was introduced to a petite, attractive woman named Lorna who was about 8 or 9 years younger than me. She had red hair and was pretty darn attractive. We just seemed to click immediately. I started calling her and we began going everywhere together—the Eagles, out to dinner, up to the mountains for picnics. I wasn't wealthy, but I did have a good pension, some savings, quite a bit of property, and a fairly new car. So I guess I was a real catch in her eyes. I certainly thought she was a catch and began thinking I might want to get remarried.

My kids were worried as Lorna had been married twice before and was now divorced. I'll admit that bothered me a little as my wife and I had been married many years and frowned on the idea of divorce. Lorne also had three kids of her own, grown ones, who were always very nice to me whenever we met. Still my kids kept warning me that Lorna was only after my money, but I just thought they were jealous or that they didn't like me dating someone else after their mother died. But they were right. I had a couple of houses and some acreage and decided to put the names of my kids on the deeds along with mine. When I casually mentioned this fact to Lorna, she immediately stopped seeing me. Wouldn't take any of my phone calls and stopped coming to the dances. I guess the kids were right; she was interested in me only for what I owned. Luckily for me and my kids, I didn't lose anything financially, but it certainly hurt my ego.

This man was fortunate that he didn't get caught, like many other widowers, in a sweetheart swindle and then find out that he had been separated from his assets through emotional manipulation.

Occasionally individuals appear to gang up on a victim. An 88-year-old widower bought a new home a year after his wife died and paid $100,000 in cash for it. The lady who had owned the home, a two-time widow named Dorothea, visited the elderly man frequently and, over a period of some months, became a very close friend. She seemed to take the man's welfare to heart and, when she saw he had dental problems, referred him to her dentist. Also, she arranged for him to be included in a Meals on Wheels program that provided lunch on a daily basis, and she occasionally supplemented this with something she had cooked that the two of them could share.

As the elderly man became more feeble and more dependent on Dorothea, she began coming to his home a portion of each day, doing some light housework and taking care of his monthly financial matters. Eventually, she persuaded the man to purchase a new car—a Cadillac Seville—which she soon appropriated for her own use. Shortly thereafter, a niece of the aged man appeared on the scene and spent a great deal of time with the couple. In the course of a few months, the niece and Dorothea became very good friends.

Although the man's sister had been named as personal representative for his will, Dorothea convinced the man that he should delete the name of his sister, name the niece in her place, and provide the niece with a power of attorney. Once this was done, it was only a matter of a few months before the man's assets disappeared—all accomplished legally by the two women using the power of attorney. The victim was left with only a small pension from social security and soon was forced to move into an assisted living residence. Deciding to purchase that particular house from that particular owner proved disastrous for this gentleman.

Sometimes one can lose more than money. One recently retired Toronto man took a new bride who almost immediately had him charged and imprisoned on a bogus assault charge. Neighbors and friends came to his rescue and bailed him out of jail, but when he returned home, he discovered that his bride had sold his house and furniture through a power of attorney that he had given her.[9] The police apprehended the bride just before take-off in a jet bound for Poland; still, his assets were gone, and he lamented the fact that he would leave his four children little in the way of inheritance.

Today many elderly people who enter into a second marriage do so with a prenuptial agreement. In this way each can protect the assets he or she brings into the union. As one man's daughter explained, "I knew that my mom had some stocks and bonds of her own that she had inherited from her parents and that it would be divided between my sister and me when dad died. Also, there was some really nice jewelry. We weren't against Dad remarrying, but we asked him to do a pre-nup because his new wife had two kids, and we didn't want them to get what we knew would be our inheritance."

Remarriage may not be the answer for all elderly, and today an ever-increasing number of seniors are "playing house"—cohabiting, in other words. An example of this is Helen Smith, 77, who became a widow in 1988. In 1995 she met a widower, and they now live together. "I love him," she said, "but I have no plans to marry him."[10]

The census bureau indicates that the number of households made up of two unrelated adults, a man and a woman, at least one of whom is 65 or older, has more than doubled since 1989. This equates to 266,000 couples but may be considerably higher because many unmarried individuals are reluctant to admit their cohabitation, even though the social stigma against this practice has eased somewhat. However, some financial problems may surface with these arrangements. If one dies without a will and all assets are in that person's name, what happens to the other partner? If partners have purchased a home together and one dies, will the survivor have to move from the home if the late individual's relatives want their share of the property? Whether or not a death is involved, have their separate belongings been cataloged? In the case that either partner wishes to have second thoughts about the arrangement, battles have erupted over ownership of furniture, paintings, pets, and so forth. Even lesser issues, such as who pays what portion of a cruise vacation, can cause a breach in the partnership.[11]

INTERNET DATING

It used to be that people looked "across a crowded room" (as the old song goes) and saw someone who they felt could fulfill all of their dreams. Today, people do not have to physically meet someone to find true love or, as happens all too often, to get ripped off in a love scam.

With the advent of the Internet and access to computers now financially feasible for so many people, older Americans are enthusiastically embracing Internet dating through such Web sites as Match.com and Yahoo.[12] Just a few minutes in a chat room can lead individuals to others seeking companionship.

Speed dating has become popular among the young. An individual meets others at a bar or restaurant, is given a list of eight or more "dates," and spends only a few minutes chatting with each. Then the individual marks on the list who he or she would like to see again, and the organizer of the event coordinates the people into pairs. This type of dating has also become popular with those 50 and older, and more groups are adding "50-plus nights."[13]

Unfortunately, as with advertisements in a newspaper or magazine, the speed daters and Cyber-Romeos are complete strangers. They don't come with a seal of approval, such as "He's a friend of your brother's," "He works with a colleague," or "We've known him and his family for years." Therefore, the unwary person may be in danger of becoming a "love victim."

Stopping these love scams is extremely difficult. First, individuals are loathe to come to grips with the fact that they are not loved, but are merely victims. They are seeking love so desperately that their fragile mental or physical health may not withstand this reality. Second, some may be too embarrassed and simply refuse to report the scam. When they do file a report, often they will not press charges. As one woman indicated, "I just want to forget that this even happened." On the other hand, a man still hated to do anything that "would hurt my little wife. She was so good to me, and I still love her." Then, too, pressing charges may be a moot point as the "lovers" are usually quick to leave an area and begin their "sweet talk" on a new victim in another locale. Also, district attorneys may be unable to prosecute if the perpetrators are found as, more times than not, the victims have given the scam artists cash, property, or other legal rights to their assets. Sometimes the only way to file a charge is to locate and name multiple victims. Still, it's hard for those who have willingly given their hearts to someone to come forth and admit they were foolish.

Where, then, does the elderly man or woman look for love? Sometimes adult children can play cupid by helping their single parent find a mate. Cupid's Coach, a matchmaking service in Southern California, indicated that inquiries on behalf of parents doubled in its second year of business. One of the nation's largest dating services, The Right One/Together, has seen a boom in its business due to kids purchasing memberships for their parents. NBC had hundreds of adult children willing to "help their single fathers find a mate for *Who Wants to Marry My Dad?*, a summer reality series."[14] Naturally, not all of the dates or matches work out, and there is always some risk in this kind of endeavor. Still, the opportunity to find that right person keeps many individuals involved.

There is no guaranteed safe place to seek companionship, but along with those already mentioned are special-interest services where singles can meet other singles with like interests. Connections are also made through groups that set up high school or college class reunions. And, even through it may sound a like something out of the eighteenth century, there is still the matchmaker. For those interested in privacy as they seek a companion, Zelda Fischer's Gentlepeople charges from $15,000 to $50,000 to set up a match. She justifies the charges by saying, "Our clients don't want to see 300 [people]; they want the one right person."[15]

Fischer's statement sums up the whole problem. Each of the elderly persons left alone is hoping to find a Mr. or Ms. Right to become their significant other. Getting back into the dating mode is usually the only way to do this. However, individuals should not be hasty or careless in their quest, and there are some red flags that should alert the wary: unwillingness to give a home or cell phone number, to extend an invitation to his or her home, to produce any family members, and to discuss any aspect of an occupation. A request for money or expensive gifts early in the relationship and a vow of undying love should signal individuals to use caution.[16] Although it sounds unromantic, a credit report on this individual or even a background check may be in order, especially if one is becoming more and more involved in a relationship.

Also, there are other precautions one can take to stay both emotionally and financially secure. Feel free to remain anonymous, even if the other person encourages revelations. Do not reveal identifying details, particularly financial details. Look for small inconsistencies in the e-mail messages sent to see if they are contradictory. Request a photo. If the lover is reluctant to send one, this may be a red flag, according to Trish McDermott, vice president of the established dating service Match.com.[17]

Inviting a potential Ms. or Mr. Right into one's home for a visit to get better acquainted may also be folly, as both emotional and financial situations may arise which could be difficult to control. If an individual pushes for a face-to-face meeting, be cautious. Try and arrange to spend a few days in a neutral setting—at a resort or some convention—where neither has made too great a commitment. Then, if things don't go as well as anticipated, a graceful exit is possible.

Taking these precautions may seem uncaring or mercenary, but individuals are making choices that will have major consequences to their lives—good or bad. After doing a bit of checking, if everything seems honest, go ahead with plans. Companionship is necessary for both good physical and emotional health. Many men and women find happiness in their golden years without ever encountering the problems mentioned earlier. Still, Trish McDermott applies to romantic involvement what President Reagan said when talking about Soviet disarmament: "Trust but verify."

Chapter Eight

Preventing Scams

---

* * *

Unfortunately scams are a cruel aspect
of the fabric of our society.
—Chuck Whitlock, *Scam School*

* * *

T he comment from the above author is certainly true. Con artists are able to continually find that easy mark and rob individuals, particularly the elderly, of their means of
subsistence, self-esteem, and trust. Warnings to the public are generally ignored by the elderly and their families. The attitude seems
to be that scams happen to everyone else. Unfortunately, millions
of seniors are scammed daily all across America.

In 2003, the *Associated Press* (along with many other media
sources) published a few guidelines to try to help those senior citizens protect themselves against fraud:

- Check out strangers touting strange deals that involve
  finances.
- If approached by a stranger, try to obtain identifying information such as car description and license number, individual description, and so forth.
- Don't let strangers into the home; keep door locked.

- Stay in charge of money, and beware of putting money into something you don't fully understand.
- Be wary of salespeople who prey on fears or indicate that money must be paid immediately because this clouds good judgment.
- Never pay for a service or product in advance from someone traveling through the area.
- Don't make rash financial decisions if a tragedy occurs, such as the death or hospitalization of a spouse or loved one.
- Don't let embarrassment or fear keep one from reporting a scam or a suspected scam.
- Prevent identity theft by shredding important documents that contain personal information.
- Do not give personal information to telemarketers. Just say no to unwanted telephone solicitations, and place names on the Do Not Call list.

These tips are valuable for all members of the public attempting to avoid con artists. However, senior citizens may feel especially vulnerable to scams as they often have limited contacts outside their homes and do not know where to turn for help. There are numerous agencies available that provide information about various scams and assist those individuals who have been scammed. These are listed in alphabetical order, not in order of importance. *Still, if fraud has occurred, call the local police department immediately.* The sooner a scam is reported, the better the chances of the con artists being apprehended and, possibly, restitution being made to a victim.

American Association of Retired Persons (AARP)
601 E Street, NW
Washington, DC 20049
1-202-434-2277 or 202-434-6030

AARP provides information to senior citizens regarding prevention of all types of fraud—investment, health, insurance, home repair, and so forth.

Better Business Bureau (BBB)

Most towns of any size have such a bureau. It educates the public regarding businesses or individuals who may be involved in fraudulent practices and works to arbitrate consumer complaints. The telephone number for the BBB is usually listed in the white pages of local telephone books.

Consumer's Resource Handbook
U.S. Office of Consumer Affairs
Consumer Information Center
Pueblo, CO 81009

This handbook provides tips on how to protect privacy and prevent credit card fraud and identity theft. If this occurs, individuals should contact all three of the following agencies.

Equifax, Inc.
P. O. Box 740123
Atlanta, GA 30374-0123

Experian
Consumer Opt-Out
701 Experian Parkway
Allen, TX 75013

Trans Union
Marketing List Opt-Out
P. O. Box 97328
Jackson, MS 39288-7328

District Attorney's Office

Many district attorney's offices have a consumer fraud division. Check the local telephone book for that agency's number.

Federal Bureau of Investigation (FBI)

The FBI investigates all federal crimes, including fraud. Check under U.S. Government in the local telephone book.

Federal Trade Commission (FTC)
Bureau of Consumer Protection
600 Pennsylvania Avenue, NW
Washington, DC 20580
1-877-382-4357 or use the online complaint form.

The FTC processes identity theft and other fraud-related complaints and publishes information to help consumers spot and avoid scams.

Internal Revenue Service (IRS)
1111 Constitution Avenue NW, Room 3244
Washington, DC 20224
1-800-829-1040

Consumers may file complaints with the IRS against deceptive charitable organizations. Address complaints to commissioner.

National Fraud Information Center (NFIC)
P. O. Box 65868
Washington, DC 20035
1-800-876-7060

The NFIC offers information on current major frauds and counselors to assist those who have been defrauded file complaints.

U.S. Postal Inspection Service
1-800-372-8347

Call the Mail Fraud Complaint Center at the number listed above if you have received a fraudulent solicitation through the mail or if you have been scammed by a mailbox bandit. Common mail scams are chain letters, pyramid schemes, charitable solicitations, Nigerian letters, and so forth.

Resources available in each state

Attorney general's office
City police department
County sheriff's department
Social services department
State banking association

Although there are many different agencies that can assist the elderly who may become victims of scams, the best way to prevent fraud is for everyone to try to protect the senior citizen. Be aware of what is happening around your neighborhood or in your apartment building. Merely being aware of anything that seems out of the ordinary and reporting it can prevent someone from suffering heavy financial losses. Elderly individuals often become isolated from family, friends, and neighbors and can be victimized. For example, one 92-year-old unmarried woman (let's call her Maude) had no relatives except for an elderly cousin living in a nearby state. Maude was still living alone in her own home but had been briefly hospitalized twice for some mental health problems. Unable to care for her yard and occasional household repairs, she hired two men to help her out. Seldom was Maude outside her home during the winter months; however, when the weather became milder, she would appear for a few minutes on the lawn. One day she approached a neighbor and during a brief conversation mentioned that she had bought a new car for one of the yardmen. The neighbor (who was in her late 80s) became concerned about this information and reported it to her daughter, who called the local social services office. When this agency checked, they discovered that the elderly woman had paid cash for the car and that it had been registered in her yardman's name. (They also found that she was paying an exorbitant price for her yard work.) Although there was nothing they could do about the auto purchase because it was a legal transaction, social services began to check on the woman weekly to try to prevent her from again becoming involved in what they considered a scam. Without the alert neighbor's involvement, who knows what further financial loss Maude would have suffered.

As with Maude's case, nothing can be done to totally prevent fraud. It has been around (as Chuck Whitlock writes in *Scam School*) since "some early caveman probably sold dinosaur dung as homemade apple pie." However, making the aged and their families aware of the potential for fraud may reduce the number of victims.

Glossary

Advance Fee Scheme: Collecting fees in advance for services or products without ever intending to fulfill the agreement.

Bait and Switch: Advertising a low-cost item and then steering the customer to a higher-priced item, claiming the low-priced item has been sold out.

Bank Examiner Scheme: A con poses as a bank examiner trying to catch a dishonest teller. Victims are encouraged to withdraw a substantial sum from their accounts to test the teller. The bank examiner asks the victims to hand over the cash for a receipt while the examiner uses the cash as evidence. The examiner then disappears with the cash, and the receipt is worthless.

Binary Compensation Program: A promotional term used to describe a pyramid scheme.

Boiler Room Operation: Attempts to sell worthless securities (or similar assets) over the telephone through high-pressure sales tactics. Although the money or credit card of the victims is billed, nothing of value is received.

Chain Letter: Letters with names listed, claiming that recipients of the letter should remove the top name on the list, put his or her name on the list, send a nominal amount of money, and mail a new list to friends/acquaintances. The claim is that individuals will receive a lot of riches in the mail, usually with a warning of bad luck if individuals "break the chain."

Charity Room: Telefunding where usually less than 10%, if any, of money raised goes to legitimate charities.

Cold Calling: Unsolicited outgoing telephone calls to potential customers whose names are usually purchased by boiler room owners.

Con: Short form of confidence game; also used to mean confidence man.

Confidence Game: Fraud scheme where perpetrator gains confidence of the mark for purpose of defrauding. (Usually, marks do not report these to law enforcement for fear of appearing foolish or because confidence game has led them to act illegally.)

Cyber Crime: Theft perpetrated through use of computers.

Dumpster Diving: Sorting through dumpsters or trashcans to obtain personal and financial information of potential victims.

Forgery: Creation of false documents or altering existing documents, especially financial instruments or other authorizations.

Fraud: Theft, concealment, or conversion for personal gain of another's money, physical assets, information, or time.

Hard Gift: An extra gift given in addition to the "gimmie gift." Also of little value.

Identity Theft: Taking victim's name, credit, and financial holdings.

Jamaican Switch: Switch of phony dollars for victim's real dollars.

Mark: Intended victim of a confidence game or swindle.

Nigerian Letter: Fraud scheme (including fax and e-mail versions) of a letter from a supposed official in Nigeria. The official supposedly has a large sum of money to transfer out of Nigeria; however, due to exchange controls, the official asks for the victim's help with the transfer. A hefty reward/commission is offered for the victim to furnish Nigerian officials with the victim's bank account number. The perpetrator depletes the victim's bank account.

Pigeon Drop: Fraud scheme involving a wallet/purse/envelope that supposedly contains a large sum of money but no identification. The perpetrator and accomplice, together with the victim, "find" the wallet. The victim is persuaded to withdraw a sum of money as "good faith" to share in the cache. The victim is distracted while the perpetrators steal the victim's money and disappear.

Ponzi Scheme: Fraud in which a high rate of return is promised on investments. The first few investors receive a high rate of return from part of the investments of later victims. At no time is any actual investment made.

Pyramid Scheme: Commercial version of the Chain Letter scheme. Fraudster sells bogus distributorships, franchises, or business opportunity plans to victims who are induced to do the same. (See also Multi-Level Marketing.)

Shill: Person in a confidence game acting as a participant to draw in the mark. An accomplice paid to play as part of a swindle. (Derived from casino gambling where a shill is a paid employee used to attract other gamblers.)

Swindle: Scheme to obtain money by ruse or false pretense. (See also Confidence Game.)

Notes

CHAPTER 1

1. Statement of Senator Joseph R. Biden, Jr., ranking member, Subcommittee on Crime, Corrections, and Victims' Rights, hearing on "Elder Abuse, Neglect, and Exploitation: Are We Doing Enough?" September 24, 2003, http://judiciary.senate.gov/member_statement.cfm?id=935&wit_id=97.

2. Testimony of W. Lee Hammond, AARP board member, Senate Executive Session: Aging, hearing on Financial Abuse and Exploitation, October 29, 2003, http://health.senate.gov/testimony/104.tes.html.

3. "Work-At-Home Scams," AARP Web site, http://www.aarp.org/consumerprotect/-frauds/Articles/a2002-20-302-FraudsWorkatHome.html (accessed March 5, 2004).

4. Fay Faron, *Rip-Off: A Writer's Guide to Crimes of Deception* (Cincinnati, Ohio: Writer's Digest Books, 1999), 7.

5. "Sleight of Hand and Other Street Scams,"http://www.crimes-of-persuasion.com/Crimes/InPerson/street-scams.html (accessed April 10, 2002).

6. "Protecting Families," *Pueblo (Colorado) Chieftain*, August 12,2003, 4A.

7. "Lottery Ticket Scammers Fool Another Victim," *Pueblo (Colorado) Chieftain*, August 16, 2001, 3B.

8. James Amos, "Lottery Ticket Scam Works Again," *Pueblo (Colorado) Chieftain*, November 16, 2002, 8A.

9. *Ibid*.

10. "Protecting Families."

11. *Ibid*.

12. Amy Matthews, "Would-be Victim Doesn't Miss Beat in Avoiding Scam," *Pueblo (Colorado) Chieftain*, October 9, 2003, 3B.

13. "Popular Con Games and How to Recognize Them," April 10, 2002, http://home.flash.net/_bpb001/congames.html; "Bank Examiner Scams," AARP Web site, http://www.aarp.org/confacts/money/bankexamine.html (accessed April 9, 2002).

14. Darla McFarland, "Scam Artist Was Posing as Officer," *(Independence, MO) Examiner*, http://examiner.net/stories/062802/new_062802008.shtml (accessed December 3, 2002).

15. "Sleight of Hand and Other Street Scams."

16. *Ibid.*

17. "Work-at-Home Scams," National Consumers League's Fraud Information Center, http://www.fraud.org.tips/telemarketing/workathome.htm (accessed March 5, 2004).

18. Robert L. Fitzpatrick, "The Growth, Acceptance, and Legalization of Pyramid Schemes: Why Women Join: It's Not Just Greed," http://www.falseprofits.com/WhyWomenJoin.html (accessed December 18, 2003). Fitzpatrick is the coauthor of *False Profits* and appeared on a May 9, 1999, *60 Minutes* program that emphasized the prosecution of those involved in illegal pyramid schemes.

19. *Ibid.*

20. Judy Hedding, "Internet Urban Legends: How to Recognize and Avoid Scams, Frauds, and Bad Guys," http://phoenix.about.com/library/weekly.aa051001j.htm (accessed December 12, 2003).

21. *Ibid.*

22. "Chain Letters," U.S. Postal Inspection Service, http://www.usps.com/websites/depart/inspect/chainlet.htm (accessed December 15, 2003).

23. "Buyers Clubs," National Consumers League's Internet Fraud Watch, http://www.fraud.org/tips/internet/buyers.htm (accessed December 12, 2003).

24. "Scammed: Psychic Shenanigans?" November 8, 2002, CBSNEWS.com, http://www.cbsnews.com/stories/2002/11/08/48hours/printable528655.shtml.

25. *Ibid.*

26. *Ibid.*

27. Joe Nickell, "The Gypsies' 'Great Trick,'" Committee for the Scientific Investigation of Claims of the Paranormal, March 1999, http://www.csicop.org/sb/9903/i-files.html (accessed December 15, 2003).

28. Comments by Robert Biancato, President of the National Committee for the Prevention of Elder Abuse, in Executive Session of Subcommittee on Aging, hearing on Financial Abuse and Exploitation, October 29, 2003, http://health.senate.gov/testimony/103_tes.html.

29. Elder Justice Act of 2003 (s.333), National Center on Elder Abuse, http://www.elderabusecenter.org/default.cfm?p=elderjustice.cfm.

30. "Sleight of Hand and Other Street Scams."

CHAPTER 2

1. Richard Titus, Fred Heinzelmann, and John M. Boyle, "The Anatomy of Fraud: Report of a Nationwide Survey," *National Institute of Justice Journal*, August 1995, 29.

2. *Ibid.*, 32.

3. Fred Joseph, "It's a New Year! Now Vow to Not Get Scammed," *Senior Beacon* 20, no. 6 (January 2002, 1).

4. Rosemary K. Breckler, *If You're over 50 You Are the Target* (San Leandro, CA: Bristol Publishing Enterprises, Inc., 1991), 205–206.

5. Titus, Heinzelmann, and Boyle, "Anatomy of Fraud," 31.

6. "Home Repair Scams," Police Department of Edison, New Jersey, http://www.seniorcitizens.com/scams/ (accessed December 4, 2001).

7. "The House of Con Games: Auto & Home Repair Schemes," http://www.geocities.com/king_grifter/autohome.html (accessed 2003).

8. "DA Is Worried About Increase in Consumer Fraud Complaints," *Pueblo (Colorado) Chieftain*, November 29, 2001, 12.

9. "Frauds, Scams and Con Games: Home Improvement Frauds," Texas Crime Prevention Association, http://www.topa/frauds/HomeImprovementFrauds.html (accessed October 3, 2003).

10. "Alleged Home Repair Fraud Incident in Rowan County," North Carolina Division of Aging, http://www.dhhs.state.nc.us/aging/fraud/alert34.htm (accessed April 4, 2002).

11. *Ibid.*

12. Senator William S. Cohen, *Easy Prey* (New York: Marlowe & Company, 1997), 35–36.

13. Kit R. Roane, "Con Artists Prey on Elderly Homeowners," *New York Times*, March 28, 1998.

14. Norma Paz Garcia, "Dirty Deeds: Abuses and Fraudulent Practices in California's Home Equity Market," Consumers Union, October 1995, http://www.consunion.org/contact.htm.

15. *Ibid.*

16. *Ibid.*

17. "Drain Patrol Sued for Grand Theft and Elder Abuse," *Reeves Journal*, 83, February 2003, 14.

18. David R. Simon, *Elite Deviance*, 7th ed. (Boston: Allyn and Bacon, 2002), 164.

19. Ibid., 164–165.

20. Cohen, Easy Prey, 49–50.

21. *Ibid.*, 46–47.

22. "Consumer Fraud Alert," Royal Canadian Mounted Police, http://www.rcmp-grc.gc.ca/scams/cfraud.htm (accessed October 16, 2003).

23. "Avoiding Home Equity Scams," Federal Trade Commission Consumer Alert, January 1988, http://www.ftc.gov/bcp/conline/pubs/alerts/eqtyalrt.htm.

24. "The 'Dirty Dozen': IRS Warns of 12 Common Scams," IRS News Release, no.2002-12, January 31, 2002, 2.

25. Dennis M. Marlock, *How to Become a Professional Con Artist* (Boulder, CO: Paladin Press, 2001), 97.

26. "Distraction Burglary: Schemes, Scams, Frauds," http://www.crimes-of-persuasion.com/Crimes/InPerson/distraction-burglary.htm (accessed April 10, 2002).

27. Stanton E. Samenow, *Inside the Criminal Mind* (New York: Crown Publishers, 1984), 93.

28. *Ibid.*

29. "Tips on Telephone Service Scams," National Fraud Information Center, December 12, 2003, http://www.fraud.org/telemarketing/teletips/telfraud.htm; Judy Hedding, "Slamming and Cramming Scams," Arizona Attorney General's Office, December 12, 2003.

30. On November 20, 2002, the sheriff's department in Pueblo, Colorado, alerted all county employees to this scam.

31. Judy Hedding, "Lacking an Original Thought Just Now?" http://phoenix.about.com/cs/scam1/a/809scam.htm (accessed December 12, 2003).

32. Titus, Heinzelmann, and Boyle, "Anatomy of Fraud," 32.

33. Patrick Malone, "Parolee Gets 144 Years for Thefts from Elderly," *Pueblo (Colorado) Chieftain*, March 5, 2004, 7A.

34. "Introducing a New Program to Help Older Coloradans," *AARP ElderWatch*, September, 2001, 1.

35. *Ibid.*, 1–2.

36. *Ibid.*; "Safer Seniors," National Crime Prevention Council, www.ncpc.org.

37. Scott Reeves, "No-Call List Puts Sales Back on Street," *Denver Post*, November 11, 2003, 1C.

CHAPTER 3

1. "Frauds and Scams: Protect Yourself and Your Money," Federal Reserve Bank of San Francisco, http://www.frbsf.org/publications/consumer/fraud.html (accessed April 10, 2002).

2. Pat Craig, "Elder Abuse: Title VII Elder Rights Protection," *Senior Beacon*, July 2003, 3.

3. "Catch the Bandit in Your Mailbox," *Senior Living*, http://seniorliving.about.com/library/newsbytes/bl_bandit_in_mailbox.htm (accessed November 26, 2001).

4. Frank W. Abagnale, *The Art of the Steal* (New York: Broadway Books, 2001), 120.

5. "Internet Fraud Lurks in Your Inbox: Nigerian Money Offer Email Is Fastest Growing Con," May 22, 2002, http://www.nclnet.org/emailscamspr02.htm.

6. "ABCs of Small Business," http://www.abcsmallbus.com/bizbasics/misc/nigerian_letter.html (accessed October 17, 2003).

7. *Ibid.*

8. David Ruppe, "Too Good to Be True,"http://abcnews.go.com/sections/world/DailyNews/nigeriafraud_000901.html (accessed October 17, 2003).

9. *Ibid.*

10. This post card was received by the authors and numerous other postal patrons in Colorado.

11. Judy Morley, "Scams Against the Elderly," from an unpublished paper, University of Southern Colorado, November 16, 2001, 6–7.

12. *Ibid.*, 7.

13. *Ibid.*

14. "Sweepstakes Fraud," Department of Justice *Consumer's Notebook*, http://www.ag.state.la.us/publications/sweepstakesfraud.htm (accessed November 27, 2002).

15. "Charity Fraud," Department of Justice *Consumer's Notebook*, http://www.ag.state.la.us/publications/charityfraud.htm (accessed November 27, 2002).

16. "Top Ten Investment Scams," North Carolina Division of Aging, http://www.dhhs.state.nc.us/aging/fraud/alert22.htm (accessed April 2002).

17. "Attorney General Salazar Announces Win in Estate Planning Consumer Fraud Case Targeting Elderly Victims Against Colorado Springs Attorney and His Associates," December 2, 2003, http://www.ago.state.co.us/PRESREL/presr12003/prsr198.htm.; "Injunction Against Estate Planning Scheme Ordered," http://www.ago.state.co.us/PRESREL/presr12002/prsr109.htm (accessed December 2, 2003); Mike Garrett, "Scam Targets Seniors in Trinidad," *Pueblo (Colorado) Chieftain*, November 7, 2001, 4B; "Illicit Estate-Planning Seminars Shut Down," *AARP Bulletin*, December 2003, 8.

18. Steven K. Paulson, "Attorney General Wins Judgment Against 2 in Estate Planning Scam," *Pueblo (Colorado) Chieftain*, February 7, 2004, 7A.

19. *Ibid.*

20. *Ibid.*

21. David Yeske, "Home-Equity Debt: Don't Use Your Home as a Checkbook," *Military Officer*, 1, no. 10, October 2003, 48.

22. Walt Duna, "Homeowners Gain: California Company to Pay $60 Million to Borrowers in 18 States After AARP Lawsuit," *AARP Bulletin*, May 2002, 18; "A Case That Really Hit Home," *AARP Magazine*, May/June, 2003, 87.

23. Carole Fleck, "Credit Repair Ripoffs," *AARP Bulletin*, March 2003, 26.

24. Anuradha Raghunathan, "Good-Looking Deals Hide Financial Snares," *(Colorado Springs) Gazette*, September 1, 2003, Business 1–2.

25. Leigh Strope, "Beware of 'Dirty Dozen': Common Scams Against Taxpayers," *Pueblo (Colorado) Chieftain*, February 20, 2003, 5C.

26. "Project Mailbox IV for Consumers: Catch the Bandit in Your Mailbox," December 3, 2002, http://www.ftc.gov/bcp/conline/edcams/mailbox/index.html.

27. "Opting Out," http://www.ftc.gov/bcp/conline/edscams/gettingcredit/optingout.html (accessed September 3, 2003).

28. Daniel Mihalko, inspector in charge, United States Postal Service, testimony before the Senate Subcommittee on Crime, Corrections and Victims' Rights, September 24, 2003.

29. "Government Moves to Stamp Out Mail Fraud," October 1, 1998 (from *Today on CNN*), CNN.com.

CHAPTER 4

1. "Let's Go Shopping, Real Stories," Federal Trade Commission, www.consumer.gov.

2. "ID Theft: When Bad Things Happen to Your Good Name," Federal Trade Commission, http://www.ftc.gov/bcp/conline/pubs/credit/idtheft.htm (accessed December 3, 2002); "Fraud?" Department of Justice, http://www.usdoj.gov/criminal/fraud/idtheft.html (accessed March 5, 2003).

3. Carole Fleck, "Stealing Your Life," *AARP Bulletin*, February 2004, 3.

4. "Fraud: 551 in Denver Were Victims of Identity Theft," *(Denver, CO) Rocky Mountain News*, January 23, 2003, 6B; Dave Pettinari, "Local Credit Card Scam Alert," *Senior Beacon*, February 2004, 22.

5. "Fraud: 551 in Denver Were Victims of Identity Theft."

6. Jonathan D. Salant, "Identity Theft Losses Greater Than Expected," *Pueblo (Colorado) Chieftain*, September 4, 2003, 5C; Bruce and Muriel Tew, "Identity Theft on the Rise: $5 Billion in Out-of-Pocket!" *Senior Beacon*, December 2003, 3.

7. "ID Theft Sticks 17-Year-Old with $30,000 Debt," *Pueblo (Colorado) Chieftain*, January 30, 2003, 2B.

8. Federal Trade Commission cases are taken from the booklet *ID Theft: When Bad Things Happen To Your Good Name*, Federal Trade Commission, September 2002 or FTC Web site www.consumer.gov/idtheft.

9. Patricia Barry, "Thieves Get Rick Quick by Stealing Your Identity," *AARP Bulletin*, November 1999, http://www.aarp.org/bulletin/nov99/theft.html.

10. *Ibid*.

11. Adam Clymer, "Elderly's Homes Lost to ID Theft," *Denver Post*, May 28, 2002, 3A.

12. *Ibid*.

13. "Identity Theft," *Pueblo (Colorado) Chieftain*, January 3, 2003, 2B.

14. "Mail Scam Targets Poor, Elderly: Scam Used to Steal Money, Identity," Click10.com (accessed October 2003).

15. "Identity Theft," *Upper Arkansas Military Retiree Sub-Council of Fort Carson*, July–August 2002, 2.

16. Fleck, "Stealing Your Life," 4.

17. "ID Theft: What's It All About?" Federal Trade Commission, May 2003, 5.

18. Bernard Stamler, "Urban Tactics: Artists Pro and Con with a New Generation of Swindles," *New York Times*, June 11, 2000.

19. Laurie Kellman, "Identity Theft Battle Frustrates Officials," *Pueblo (Colorado) Chieftain*, July 31, 2002, 8A.

20. "Ten Tips to Prevent Credit Card Fraud," *Consumer's Notebook*, Department of Justice: Credit Card Fraud, http://www.ag.state.la.us/publications/creditcardfraud.htm (accessed November 27, 2002); "Identity Theft: What You Should Know," AARP Web site, http://www.aarp.org/confacts/money/identity.html (accessed April 9, 2002).

21. "Identity Theft and Fraud," U.S. Department of Justice, http://www.usdoj/gov/criminal/fraud/idtheft.html (accessed March 5, 2004).

22. *Ibid*.

23. Ruth Simon, "Identity-Theft Protection Firms Get Lift," *Denver Post*, November 29, 2002, 4C.

24. Joanne Cleaver, "Identity Crisis," *Friendly Exchange*, Spring 2002, 15.

25. *Ibid*.

26. "ID Theft Victims Can Alert Creditors, Police with One Call," *Pueblo (Colorado) Chieftain*, October 29, 2003, 10A.

CHAPTER 5

1. Testimony of Daniel L. Mihalko, United States Postal Inspection Service, before the Senate Subcommittee on Crime, Corrections and Victims' Rights, September 24, 2003, http://judiciary.senate.gov//testimony.cfm?id=935&wit_id=2650.

2. "Telemarketing Fraud Statistics," National Fraud Information Center, http://www.fraud.org/02telestats.htm (accessed October 17, 2002); *Consumer's Notebook*, Department of Justice: Telemarketing Fraud, http://www.ag.state.la.us/publications/telemarketingfraud.htm (accessed November 27, 2002); Alan S. Kopit, consumer attorney, "How to Spot Holiday Scams: Tips to Help Seniors Avoid Becoming Victims," MSNBC Explorer, http://msnbc.msn.com (accessed November 27, 2001).

3. "Telemarketing Fraud Statistics."

4. "Victims of Consumer and Investment Fraud," http://www.crimes-of-persuasion.com/Victims/victims.htm (accessed October 17, 2003); Susan L. Crowley, "Boiler Room Rogues Turn on the Heat," *AARP Bulletin*, April 2000, http://www.aarp.org/bulletin/apr00/boiler.html.

5. John Nicol Ferguson, "Phone Scams: Telemarketing Fraud Is Mushrooming in North America—and Canadians Are the Villains," *Maclean's*, 111, no. 42 (1998): 12.

6. Les Henderson, *Crimes of Persuasion* (Azilda, Ontario, Canada: Coyote Ridge Publishing, 2000), 59.

7. "Examples of Telemarketing Fraud Originating in Canada," *Kansas City Star*, May 6, 2001, http:www.kansascitystar.com.

8. Myron Levin, "Canada Scam Artists Have a Global Reach," *Los Angeles Times*, July 7, 2002, C.1.

9. "Three Reasons Why . . .," *AARP ElderWatch*, September 2001, 3.

10. *Ibid*.

11. "Mutual Financial Co. Lottery Scammers Brow-Beating Seniors," http://www.dhhs.state.nc.us/aging/fraud/alert41.htm (accessed April 10, 2002).

12. Ferguson, 1–2.

13. *Ibid*., 12–13.

14. "You Have Won a Cadillac!" North Carolina Division of Aging, http://www.dhhs.state.nv.us/aging/fraud/alert33.htm (accessed April 10, 2002).

15. "Court Halts Illegal Canadian Lottery Scheme," Federal Trade Commission, http://www.ftc.gov/opa/2002/12/ems.htm (accessed December 12, 2003).

16. William S. Cohen, *Easy Prey* (New York: Marlowe & Company, 1997), 56.

17. "How to Spot Holiday Scams."

18. "Supreme Court Sets New Rule on Charity Fraud," *AARP Bulletin*, June 2003, 26.

19. "Telemarketer Accused of Fraud," *AARP Bulletin*, March 2003, 27.

20. "Telemarketing Travel Fraud," http://www.ftc.gov/bcp/conline/pubs/tmarkg/trvlfrd.htm (accessed December 4, 2001).

21. Rosemary K. Breckler, *If You're Over 50 You Are the Target* (San Leandro, CA: Bristol Publishing Enterprises, Inc., 1991), 213.

22. "Travel Travesties," *AARP Bulletin*, July–August 2003, 26.

23. Henderson, 11–12.

24. Carole Fleck, "For Some Travelers, New Red-Ink Alert," *AARP Bulletin*, June 2003, 24.

25. *Ibid*.

26. Amy Matthews, "Police Warning to Seniors: Don't Give SSN over Phone," *Pueblo (Colorado) Chieftain*, July 27, 2003, 3B.

27. "Card-Sharp Games," *AARP Bulletin*, October 2003, 24.

28. "You Have Won a Cadillac," *AARP Bulletin*, October 2003, 24.

29. "Examples of Telemarketing Fraud Originating in Canada."

30. "Credit Card Loss Protection Offers: They're the Real Steal," http://www.ftc.gov/bcp/conline/pubs/alerts/lossalrt.htm (accessed December 12, 2003).

31. Henderson, 59.

32. Joseph P. Fried, "Telemarketing Schemes Burn Twice, Taking Money and Then Selling Lists of 'Suckers,'" *New York Times*, July 8, 2001; "Slam That Telephone Scam: A Federal Crackdown Should Help Limit the Reach of Con Artists Dialing for Your Dollars. You Can Also Take Steps to Protect Yourself," *Christian Science Monitor*, March 5, 2001, 15.

33. Mihalko.

34. "Telemarketing Recovery Scams," Federal Trade Commission, http://www.ftc.gov/bcp/conline/pubs/tmarkg/recovery.htm (accessed October 17, 2003).

35. "Scam Artists Use Do Not Call Registry to Commit Fraud," Federal Trade Commission, http://www.ftc.gov/opa/2002/06/donotcallscam.htm (accessed October 27, 2003).

36. *Ibid.*

37. Deborah Powell, "On the Trail of A Telemarketing Scam," *Consumer's Research Magazine* 84 (June 2001), 34.

38. "Straight Talk About Telemarketing," Federal Trade Commission—Facts For Consumers, http://www.ftc.gov/bcp/conline/pubs/tmarkg/straight.htm (accessed October 17, 2003).

39. "How Telemarketers Work," *Air Force Times*, September 22, 2003, 46.

40. *Ibid.*

41. Linda Greider, "Hanging Up on Telemarketers," *AARP Bulletin*, November 2002, 12.

42. "Shopping by Phone: A One-Stop Guide to Consumer Protection," Federal Trade Commission, http://www.ftc.gov/bcp/conline/pubs/buying/shopping.htm (accessed December 3, 2002).

43. *Ibid.*

44. "Telemarketing Fraud," National Consumers League, http://www.fraud.org.tips/telemarketing/general.htm (accessed March 5, 2004).

CHAPTER 6

1. Robert J. Brym and John Lie, *Sociology: Your Compass for a New World* (Belmont, CA: Wadsworth, 2005), 333.

2. Ellen Hoffman, "Managing Money From Afar," *AARP Bulletin*, June 2003, 21.

3. Susan Herman, executive director, National Center for Victims of Crime, testimony before the U.S. Senate Judiciary, July 21, 1999.

4. Information taken from a General Durable Power of Attorney used in Colorado.

5. "Fighting Financial Abuse of Elderly Residents: (Santa Clara County, California)," *American City & County* 116 (December 2001): 50.

6. Joe Volz, "'Perfect Storm' for Stock Scams," *AARP Bulletin*, October 2003, 23.

7. "Top Ten Investment Schemes," North Carolina Division of Aging, http://www.dhhs.state.nv.us/aging/fraud/alert22.htm (accessed April 10, 2002).

8. Volz, 23–24; Marcy Gordon, "Con Artists Target Desperate Seniors Offering Complex Investment Scams," *(Pueblo, Colorado) Chieftain*, September 7, 2003, 1E.

9. J. Joseph Curran, Jr., Attorney General, State of Maryland, testimony before the Senate Subcommittee on Aging, Financial Abuse and Exploitation, October 30, 2003, http://health.senate.gove/testimony/099_tes.html.

10. Howard Pankratz, "Alzheimer Patient's Conservator Charged in Theft of $1.9 Million," *Denver Post*, October 8, 2003.

11. *Ibid.*

12. Latayne C. Scott, "Social inSecurity: Safeguard Your Numbers—and Your Identity," *Military Officer*, October 2003, 32.

13. Les Henderson, *Crimes of Persuasion* (Azilda, Ontario, Canada: Coyote Ridge Publishing, 2000), 274.

14. "Report Finds Abuse in US Nursing Homes Goes Unreported and Unpunished," *Lancet*, March 9, 2002, 860.

15. Ed Sealover, "Embezzler Shelled Out $200,000 on Perfume," *(Colorado Springs) Gazette*, November 19, 2003, A1, A14.

16. Carol Scott, witness, Senate Subcommittee on Aging, Financial Abuse and Exploitation, October 29, 2003, http://health.senate.gov/testimony/106_tes.html.

17. Malcolm K. Sparrow, License to Steal (Boulder, CO: Westview Press, 2000), 56.

18. Douglas Frantz, "Hospice Boom Is Giving Rise to New Fraud," *New York Times*, May 10, 1998, 18.

19. *Ibid.*

20. Sparrow, 24.

21. *Ibid.*

22. Maureen Feighan, "Woman Charged in Senior Citizen Scam," *Detroit News*, July 6, 2001.

23. "Sweetheart Swindle Scams," August 2002, http://www.crimes-of-persuasion.com/Crimes/InPerson/MajorPerson/sweetheart.htm.

24. Martine Costello, "Scams Against the Elderly," *Money*, October 13, 2000.

25. "Caretaker Charged With Bilking Elderly CU Members," *Credit Union Journal*, July 1, 2002, 2.

26. Henderson, 14–15.

CHAPTER 7

1. Mary Ann Lamanna and Agnes Riedmann, *Marriages and Families: Making Choices and Facing Change* (Belmont, CA: Wadsworth, 1994), 509–510.

2. *Ibid.*, 178–179.

3. Walter Goodman, "I Love You, You're Perfect, Now Give Me Your Money," *New York Times*, March 14, 2000, Section E, 8.

4. *Ibid.*

5. Edgar Sanchez, "Scam Alert: Man Says 'Gypsy Sweetheart Swindler' Stole His Heart—and His Cash," *Sacramento Bee*, June 10, 2003.

6. Candice Dobelstein Botner, "My Father's Journals," http://www.geocities.com/s_o_s.elderabuse/MyFathersJournals.html (accessed October 27, 2003).

7. "Sweetheart Swindle Scams," http://www.crimes-of-persuasion.com/ Crimes/InPerson/MajorPerson/sweetheart.htm (accessed June 10, 2003).

8. Fay Faron, *Rip-Off: A Writer's Guide to Crimes of Deception* (Cincinnati, Ohio: Writer's Digest Books, 1998), 98–99.

9. Nolan Young, "The Sweetheart Swindle," http://www.geocities.com/ s_o_s_elderabuse/TheSweetheartSwindle1999.html (accessed October 27, 2003).

10. Jeffrey Zaslow, "Unmarried With Grandchildren: Seniors Shacking Up Face Unexpected Issues," *Wall Street Journal*, March 4, 2004, D1.

11. *Ibid.*; Hugh O'Neill, "Come Fly With Me," *AARP Magazine*, March/April 2004, 24.

12. Sarah Mahoney, "Seeking Love," *AARP Magazine*, November/December 2003, 61–67.

13. *Ibid.*, 66.

14. When the Kids Play Cupid," *AARP Magazine*, September/October 2003, 11–12.

15. Mahoney, 66–67.

16. Nolan Young, "Q&A: Scams, Gold Diggers, and Red Flags!" http://www.aloveinrussia.com/q_n_a/scams_rf_gd.shtml
(accessed November 6, 2003).

17. Hugh O'Neill, "Hearts and Browsers," *AARP Magazine*, September/October 2003, 26.

Bibliography

Abagnale, Frank W. *The Art of the Steal: How to Protect Yourself and Your Business from Fraud, America's #1 Crime*. New York: Broadway Books, 2002.

"ABCs of Small Business." http://www.abcsmallbus.com/bizbasics/misc/nigerian_letter.html (accessed October 17, 2003).

"Alleged Home Repair Fraud Incident in Rowan County." From the North Carolina Division of Aging, http://www.dhhs.state.nc.us/aging/fraud/alert34.htm (accessed April 4, 2002).

Amos, James. "Lottery Ticket Scam Works Again." *Pueblo (Colorado) Chieftain*, November 16, 2002.

Anders, Kelly. "Financial Crimes Against the Elderly." National Conference of States, July, 1999.

"Attorney General Salazar Announces Win In Estate Planning Consumer Fraud Case Targeting Elderly Victims Against Colorado Springs Attorney and His Associates." http://www.ago.state.co.us/PRESREL/presr12003/prsr198.htm (accessed December 2, 2003).

"Avoiding Home Equity Scams." Federal Trade Commission Consumer Alert, http://www.ftc.gov/bcp/conline/pubs/alerts/eqtyalrt.htm (accessed January 1988).

"Bank Examiner Scams." AARP Webplace, http://www.aarp.org/confacts/money/bankexamine.html (accessed April 9, 2002).

Barry, Patricia. "Thieves Get Rich Quick By Stealing Your Identity." *AARP Bulletin*, November 1999, http://www.aarp.org/bulletin/nov99/theft.html.

Biancato, Robert [President of the National Committee for the Prevention of Elder Abuse]. Comments in Senate Executive Session on Aging Financial Abuse and Exploitation, October 29, 2003, http://health.senate.gove/testimony/103_tes.html.

Biden, Senator Joseph R. [Ranking Member, Subcommittee on Crime, Corrections and Victims' Rights Hearing]. Statement on "Elder Abuse, Neglect, and Exploitation: Are We Doing Enough?" September 24, 2003.

Bortnick, Barry. "Agencies Unite to Combat Scams That Prey on Elderly." *(Colorado Springs) Gazette*, April 5, 2002.

Botner, Candice Dobelstein. "My Father's Journals." http://www. geocities.com/s_o_s.elderabuse/MyFathersJournals.html (accessed October 27, 2003).

Breckler, Rosemary K. *If You're Over 50 You Are the Target*. San Leandro, CA: Bristol Publishing Enterprises, Inc., 1991.

Brownell, Patricia J. *Family Crimes Against the Elderly*. New York: Taylor & Francis, Inc., 1998.

Brym, Robert J., and John Lie. *Sociology: Your Compass for a New World*. Belmont, CA: Wadsworth, 2005.

Bureau of Justice Statistics, Table 82, Personal and Property Crimes 2002.

"Buyers Clubs." National Consumers League Fraud Watch, http://www.fraud.org/tips/internet/buyers.htm (accessed December 12, 2003).

Camille, Pamela. *Getting Older, Getting Fleeced: The National Shame of Financial Elder Abuse and How to Avoid It*. Santa Barbara, CA: Fithian Press, 1996.

"Can Someone Steal Your Identity?" Trilegiant Corporation, Trumbull, CT, 2001.

Caravella, John. *Marked for Destruction*. JP Products, 2000.

"Card-Sharp Games." *AARP Bulletin*, October 2003.

"Caretaker Charged with Bilking Elderly CU Members." *Credit Union Journal*, July 1, 2002.

"A Case That Really Hit Home." *AARP Magazine*, May/June 2003.

"Catch the Bandit in Your Mailbox." *Senior Living*, http://seniorliving.about.com/library.newsbytes/bl_bandit_in_mailbox.htm (accessed November 26, 2001).

"Chain Letters." U.S. Postal Inspection Service, http://www.usps.com/websites/depart/inspect/chainlet.htm (accessed December 15, 2003).

"Charitable Solicitations Homepage." Colorado Secretary of State, December 12, 2003, http://www.sos.state.co.us/pubs/bingo_raffles/charsolicitation1.htm.

"Charity Fraud." Department of Justice *Consumer's Notebook*, http://www.ag.state.la.us/publications/charityfraud.htm (accessed November 27, 2002).

Cleaver, Joanne. "Identity Crisis." *Friendly Exchange*, Spring 2002.

Clymer, Adam. "Elderly's Homes Lost to ID Theft." *Denver Post*, May 28, 2002.

Cohen, William S. [Senator]. *Easy Prey: The Fleecing of America's Senior Citizens—And How to Stop It*. New York: Marlowe & Co., 1997.

"Consumer Fraud Alert." Royal Canadian Mounted Police, October 16, 2003, http://www.rcmp-grc.gc.ca/scams/cfraud.htm (accessed October 16, 2003).

Consumer Fraud and the Elderly: Easy Prey? Hearing before the Special Committee on Aging, United States Senate, September 24, 1992. Washington, D.C.: U.S. G.P.O.

Consumer's Notebook. Department of Justice: Telemarketing Fraud, http://www.ag.state.la.us/publications/telemarketingfraud.htm (accessed November 27, 2002).

Costello, Martine. "Scams Against the Elderly." *Money*, October 13, 2000.

"Court Halts Illegal Canadian Lottery Scheme." Federal Trade Commission, http://www.ftc.gov/opa/2002/12/ems.htm (accessed December 12, 2002).

Craig, Pat. "Elder Abuse: Title VII Elder Rights Protection." *Senior Beacon*, July 2003.

"Credit Card Loss Protection Offers: They're the Real Steal." http://www.ftc.gov/bcp/conline/pubs/alerts/lossalrt.htm (accessed December 12, 2003).

Crowley, Susan L. "Boiler Room Rogues Turn on the Heat." *AARP Bulletin*, April 2000.

Curran, J. Joseph, Jr. [Attorney General State of Maryland]. Testimony Before Senate Subcommittee on Aging, Financial Abuse and Exploitation, October 30, 2003, http://health.senate.gov/testimony/099_tes.html.

"DA Is Worried about Increase in Consumer Fraud Complaints." *Pueblo (Colorado) Chieftain*, November 29, 2001.

Dinnen, Steve. "Slam That Telephone Scam." *Christian Science Monitor*, 2001.

"The 'Dirty Dozen': IRS Warns of 12 Common Scams." IRS News Release, No. 2002-12, January 31, 2002.

"Distraction Burglary: Schemes, Scams, Frauds." http://www.crimes-of-persuasion .com/Crimes/InPerson/distraction-burglary.htm (accessed April 10, 2002).

"Drain Patrol Sued for Grand Theft and Elder Abuse." *Reeves Journal* 83, no. 2 (February 2003).

Ducovny, Amram. *The Billion Dollar Swindle: Frauds Against The Elderly.* New York: Fleet Press Corporation, 1969.

Duna, Walt. "Homeowners Gain: California Company to Pay $60 Million to Borrowers in 18 States after AARP Lawsuit." *AARP Bulletin, May 2002.*

Elder Justice Act of 2003 (s.333). National Center on Elder Abuse, http:// www.elderabusecenter.org/default.cfm?p=elderjustice.cfm.

"E-Mail Scams—How to Recognize Advance Fee Fraud." October 17, 2003, http:// www.abcsmallbiz.com/bizbasics/misc/nigerian_letter.html.

"Examples of Telemarketing Fraud Originating in Canada." http://www.kansascitystar.com (accessed May 6, 2001).

"Fakers, Frauds and Senior Scams." April 2003, http://seniorliving.about.com/ htm?iam.

Faron, Fay. *Rip-Off: A Writer's Guide to Crimes Deception.* Cincinnati, Ohio: Writers Digest Books, 1999.

Fattah, Ezzat A. *Crime and Victimization of the Elderly.* Springer Verlag: 1989.

Feighan, Maureen. "Woman Charged in Senior Citizen Scam." *Detroit News*, July 6, 2001.

Ferguson, John Nicol. "Phone Scams: Telemarketing Fraud Is Mushrooming in North America—and Canadians Are the Villains." *Maclean's* 111 (October 19, 1998).

"Fighting Financial Abuse of Elderly Residents: (Santa Clara County, California)." *American City & County* 116, (December 2001).

Fitzgerald, Randy. "Fraud Against Aged People." *Reader's Digest* 157 (August 2000).

Fitzpatrick, Robert L. "Why Women Join: It's Not Just Greed." http:// www.falseprofits.com/WhyWomenJoin.html (accessed December 18, 2003).

Fleck, Carole. "Pills, Potions and Powders." *AARP Bulletin*, November 2001.

———. "Credit Repair Ripoffs." *AARP Bulletin*, March 2003.

———. "For Some Travelers, New Red-Ink Alert." *AARP Bulletin*, June 2003.

———. "Stealing Your Life." *AARP Bulletin*, February 2004.

Frantz, Douglas. "Hospice Boom Is Giving Rise to New Fraud." *New York Times*, May 10, 1998.

"Fraud: 551 in Denver Were Victims of Identity Theft." *Rocky Mountain News*, January 23, 2003.

"Frauds and Scams: Protect Yourself and Your Money." Federal Reserve Bank of San Francisco, http://www.frbsf.org/publications/consumer/fraud.html (accessed April 10, 2002).

"Frauds, Scams and Con Games: Home Improvement Frauds." Texas Crime Prevention Association, http://www.topa/frauds/ HomeImprovementFrauds.html (accessed October 3, 2003).

Fried, Joseph. "Telemarketing Schemes Burn Twice, Taking Money and Then Selling Lists of 'Suckers.'" *New York Times*, July 8, 2001.

Garcia, Norma Paz. "Dirty Deeds: Abuses and Fraudulent Practices in California's Home Equity Market." Consumers Union's West Coast Regional Office, October 1995, http://www.consunion.org/contact.htm.

Garrett, Mike. "Scam Targets Seniors in Trinidad." *Pueblo (Colorado) Chieftain*, November 7, 2001.

Goodman, Walter. "Television Review: I Love You, You're Perfect, Now Give Me Your Money." *New York Times*, March 14, 2000.

Gordon, Marcy. "Con Artists Target Desperate Seniors Offering Complex Investment Scams." *Pueblo (Colorado) Chieftain*, September 7, 2003.

"Government Moves to Stamp Out Mail Fraud." October 1, 1998, (From *Today* on CNN), CNN.com.

Greider, Linda. "Hanging Up On Telemarketers." *AARP Bulletin*, November 2002.

Hammond, W. Lee [AARP Board Member]. Testimony at the Senate Executive Session: Hearing on Aging, Financial Abuse and Exploitation, October 29, 2003, http://health.senate.gov/testimony/104.tes.html.

Hedding, Judy. "Internet Urban Legends: How to Recognize and Avoid Scams, Frauds and Bad Guys." http://phoenix.about.com/library/weeklyaa051001j.htm (accessed December 12, 2003).

———. "Lacking an Original Thought Just Now." http://phoenix.about.com/cs/scam1/a/809scam.htm (accessed December 12, 2003).

———. "Slamming and Cramming Scams." Arizona Attorney General's Office, December 12, 2003, http://phoenix.about.com/library/weekly/aa05100li.htm.

Henderson, Les. *Crimes of Persuasion*. Azilda, Ontario, Canada: Coyote Ridge Publishing, 2000.

Herman, Susan [Executive Director, National Center for Victims of Crime]. Testimony before the U.S. Senate Judiciary, July 21, 1999.

Hoffman, Ellen. "Managing Money from Afar." *AARP Bulletin*, June 2003.

"Home Repair Scams." Edison, New Jersey, Police Department, http://www.seniorcitizens.com/scams/ (accessed December 4, 2001).

"The House of Con Games: Auto & Home Repair Schemes." http://www.geocities.com/king_grifter/autohome.html (accessed August 2003).

"How Telemarketers Work." *Air Force Times*, September 22, 2003.

"Identity Theft." *Pueblo (Colorado) Chieftain*, January 3, 2003.

"Identity Theft." *Upper Arkansas Military Retiree Sub-Council of Fort Carson*, July–August 2002.

"Identity Theft and Fraud." U.S. Department of Justice, http://www.usdoj.gov/criminal/fraud/idtheft.html (accessed March 5, 2004).

"Identity Theft on the Rise: $5 Billion in Out-of-Pocket!" *Senior Beacon*, December 2003.

"Identity Theft: What You Should Know." http://www.aarp.org/confacts/money/identity.html (accessed April 9, 2002).

"ID Theft Sticks 17-Year-Old with $30,000 Debt." *Pueblo (Colorado) Chieftain*, January 30, 2003.

"ID Theft Victims Can Alert Creditors, Police with One Call." *Pueblo (Colorado) Chieftain*, October 29, 2003.

ID Theft: What's It All About? Federal Trade Commission, May 2003.

ID Theft: When Bad Things Happen to Your Good Name. Federal Trade Commission, http://www.usdoj.gov/criminal/fraud/idtheft.html (accessed December 3, 2002).

"Illicit Estate-Planning Seminars Shut Down." *AARP Bulletin,* December 2003.

"Injunction Against Estate Planning Scheme Ordered." http://www.ago .state.co.us/PRESREL/presr12002/prsr109.htm (accessed December 2, 2003).

"Internet Fraud Lurks in Your Inbox: Nigerian Money Offer Email Is Fastest Growing Con." May 22, 2002, http://www.nclnet.org/emailscamspr02.htm.

"Introducing a New Program to Help Older Coloradoans." *AARP Elder Watch,* September 2001.

Joseph, Fred. "It's A New Year! Now Vow to Not Get Scammed." *Senior Beacon* 20, no. 6 (January 2002).

Kellman, Laurie. "Identity Theft Battle Frustrates Officials." *Pueblo (Colorado) Chieftain,* July 31, 2002.

Kopit, Alan S. "How to Spot Holiday Scams." NBC News, MSNBC Explorer, http://msnbc.msn.com, (accessed November 27, 2001).

Lamanna, Mary Ann and Agnes Riedmann. *Marriages and Families: Making Choices and Facing Change.* Belmont, CA: Wadsworth, 1994.

"Let's Go Shopping Real Stories." Federal Trade Commission, www.consumer.gov.

Levin, Myron. "Canada Scam Artists Have a Global Reach." *Los Angeles Times,* July 7, 2002.

"Lottery Ticket Scammers Fool Another Victim," *Pueblo (Colorado) Chieftain,* August 16, 2001.

Mahoney, Sarah. "Seeking Love." *AARP Magazine,* November/December, 2003.

"Mail Scam Targets Poor, Elderly: Scam Used to Steal Money, Identity." Click10.com (accessed October 2003).

Malone, Patrick. "Parolee Gets 144 Years for Thefts from Elderly." *Pueblo (Colorado) Chieftain,* March 5, 2004.

Mannix, Margaret. "Stolen Identify." *U.S. News & World Report,* June 1, 1998.

Matthews, Amy. "Police Warning to Seniors: Don't Give SSN over Phone." *Pueblo (Colorado) Chieftain,* July 27, 2003.

————. "Would-Be Victim Doesn't Miss Beat in Avoiding Scam." *Pueblo (Colorado) Chieftain,* October 9, 2003.

Marlock, Dennis M. *How to Become a Professional Con Artist.* Boulder, CO: Paladin Press, 2001.

Maurer, David W., and Luc Sante. *The Big Con: The Story of the Confidence Man.* New York: Anchor Books, 1968.

McFarland, Darla. "Scam Artist Was Posing as Officer." *(Independence, MO) Examiner,* http://examiner.net/stories/062802/new_062802008.shtml (accessed December 3, 2002).

Mihalko, Daniel [United States Postal Service]. Statement before the Senate Subcommittee on Crime, Corrections and Victims' Rights, September 24, 2003, http://judiciary.senate.gov/testimony.cfn?id&wit_id=2650.

Morley, Judy. "Scams Against the Elder." Unpublished paper, University of Southern Colorado, November 16, 2001.

"Mutual Financial Co. Lottery Scammers Brow-Beating Seniors." http://www.dhhs.state.nc.us/aging/fraud/alert41.htm (accessed April 10, 2002).

National Center for Victims of Crime. Speeches and Testimony, remarks by Susan Herman, Executive Director, July 21, 1999, http://www.nvc.org/press/speeches/elderfraud.html.

National Fraud Information Center. 2002 Internet Fraud Statistics, http://www.fraud.org/2002instats.htm (accessed October 17, 2002).

Nickell, Joe. "The Gypsies' 'Great Trick'." Committee for the Scientific Investigation of Claims of the Paranormal, March 1999, http://www.csicop.org/sb/9903/i-files.html (accessed December 15, 2003).

Office of the Attorney General, State of Texas. "Elder Texans' Page." January 3, 2002, www.tlsc.org.

O'Neill, Hugh. "Hearts and Browsers." *AARP Magazine*, September/October, 2003.

———. "Come Fly With Me." *AARP Magazine*, March/April 2004.

"Opting Out." http://www.ftc.gov/bcp/conline/edcams/gettingcredit/optingout.html (accessed September 3, 2003).

Orsini-Meinhard, Kirsten. "Lottery Scam Persists." *Pueblo (Colorado) Chieftain*, November 25, 2002.

———. "Identity Theft Scams Hit Home." *Pueblo (Colorado) Chieftain,* November 27, 2002.

Pankratz, Howard. "Alzheimer Patient's Conservator Charged in Theft of $1.9 Million." *Denver Post*, October 8, 2003.

Paulson, Steven K. "Attorney General Wins Judgment Against 2 in Estate Planning Scam." *Pueblo (Colorado) Chieftain*, February 7, 2004.

Pettinari, Dave. "Local Credit Card Scam Alert." *Senior Beacon*, February 2004.

"The Pigeon Drop." April 9, 2001, http://www.aarp.org/confacts/money/pigeondrop.html.

"Popular Con Games and How to Recognize Them." http://home.flash.net/_bpb001/congames.htm (accessed April 10, 2002).

Powell, Deborah. "On the Trail of a Telemarketing Scam." *Consumers Research Magazine* 84 (June 2001).

"Project Mailbox IV for Consumers: Catch the Bandit in Your Mailbox." December 3, 2002, http://www.ftc.gov/bcp/conline/edcams/mailbox/index.html.

"Protecting Families." *Pueblo (Colorado) Chieftain*, August 12, 2003.

"Q&A—Scams, Gold Diggers, and Red Flags!" November 6, 2003, http://www.aloveinrussia.com/q_n_a/scans_rf_gd.shtml.

Raghunathan, Anuradha. "Good-Looking Deals Hide Financial Snares." *Gazette*, September 1, 2003.

Redding, Stan, and Frank W. Abagnale. *Catch Me If You Can: The True Story of a Real Fake*. New York: Broapdway Books, August 2000.

Reeves, Scott. "No-Call List Puts Sales Back on Street." *Denver Post*, November 11, 2003.

"Report Finds Abuse in US Nursing Homes Goes Unreported and Unpunished." *Lancet*, March 9, 2002.

"Respecting Our Elders: A Statewide Action Plan to Combat Senior Fraud." Colorado Attorney General's office, November 23, 1999.

Roane, Kit R. "Con Artists Prey on Elderly Homeowners." *New York Times*, March 28, 1998.

Ruppe, David. "Too Good to Be True." ABC News, http://Pabcnews.go.com/sections/world/DailyNews/nigeriafraud_000901.html (accessed October 17, 2003).

"Safer Seniors." National Crime Prevention Council, www.ncpc.org.

Salant, Jonathan D. "Identity Theft Losses Greater Than Expected." *Pueblo (Colorado) Chieftain*, September 4, 2003.

Samenow, Stanton E. *Inside the Criminal Mind*. New York: Crown Publishers, 1984.

Sanchez, Edgar. "Scam Alert: Man Says 'Gypsy Sweetheart Swindler' Stole His Heart—and His Cash." *Sacramento Bee*, June 10, 2003.

"Scam Alert." *AARP Bulletin*. 43, no. 7 (July–August 2002).

"Scam Artists Use Do Not Call Registry to Commit Fraud." Federal Trade Commission, October 27, 2003, http://www.ftc.gov/opa/2002/06/donotcallscam.htm.

"Scammed: Psychic Shenanigans?" November 8, 2002, CBSNEWS.com, http://www.cbsnews.com/stories/2002/11/08/48hours/printable528655.shtml.

Scott, Carol. Testimony before the Senate Subcommittee on Aging, Financial Abuse and Exploitation, October 29, 2003, http://health .senate.gov/testimony/106_tes.html.

Scott, Latayne C. "Social inSecurity: Safeguard Your Numbers—and Your Identity." *Military Officer*, October 2003.

Sealover, Ed. "Embezzler Shelled Out $200,000 on Perfume." *Gazette*, November 19, 2003.

"Shopping By Phone: A One-Stop Guide to Consumer Protection." Federal Trade Commission, http://www.ftc.gov/bcp/conline/pubs/buying/shopping.htm (accessed December 3, 2002).

Simmons, J. L. *67 Ways to Protect Seniors from Crime*. New York: Henry Holt, 1993.

Simon, David R. *Elite Deviance*. 7th ed. Boston: Allyn and Bacon, 2002.

Simon, Ruth. "Identity-Theft Protection Firms Get Lift." *Denver Post*, November 29, 2002.

"Slam That Telephone Scam: A Federal Crackdown Should Help Limit the Reach of Con Artists Dialing for Your Dollars. You Can Also Take Steps to Protect Yourself." *Christian Science Monitor*, March 5, 2001.

"Sleight of Hand and Other Street Scams." http://www .crimes-of-persuasion.com/Crimes/InPerson/street-scams.htm (accessed April 10, 2002).

Sparrow, Malcolm K. *License to Steal*. Boulder, CO: Westview Press, 2000.

Stamler, Bernard. "Urban Tactics: Artists Pro and Con with a New Generation of Swindles." *New York Times*, June 11, 2000.

"Straight Talk About Telemarketing." Federal Trade Commission—Facts for Consumers, http://www.ftc.gov/bcp/conline/pubs/tmarkg/straight.htm (October 17, 2003).

Strope, Leigh. "Beware of 'Dirty Dozen': Common Scams Against Taxpayers." *Pueblo (Colorado) Chieftain*, February 20, 2003.

"Supreme Court Sets New Rule on Charity Fraud." *AARP Bulletin*, March 2003.

"Sweepstakes Fraud." *Consumer's Notebook,* Department of Justice, http://www.ag.state.la.us/publications/sweepstakesfraud.htm (accessed November 27, 2002).

"Sweetheart Swindle Scams." http://www.crimes-of-persuasion.com/Crimes/InPerson/MajorPerson/sweetheart.htm (accessed June 10, 2003).

"Telemarketer Accused of Fraud." *AARP Bulletin*, March 2003.

"Telemarketing Fraud." National Consumers League's National Fraud Information Center, http://www.fraud.org.tips/telemarketing/general.htm (accessed March 5, 2004).

"Telemarketing Fraud Statistics." National Fraud Information Center, http://
www.fraud.org/o2telestats.htm, (accessed October 17, 2003).
"Telemarketing Recovery Scams." October 17, 2003, http://www.ftc.gov/bcp/
conline/pubs/markg/recovery.htm.
"Telemarketing Travel Fraud." http://www.ftc.gov/bcp.trvlfrd.htm (accessed
December 4, 2001).
"Ten Tips to Prevent Credit Card Fraud." *Consumer's Notebook*, Department of Jus-
tice: Credit Card Fraud, http://www.ag.state.la.us/publications/
creditcardfraud.htm (accessed November 27, 2002).
Tew, Bruce and Muriel. "Identity Theft on the Rise: $5 Billion In Out-of-Pocket?"
Senior Beacon, December 2003.
"Three Reasons Why." AARP *ElderWatch*, September 2001.
"Tips on Telephone Service Scams." National Fraud Information Center, December
12, 2003, http://www.fraud.org/telemarketing/teletips/telfraud.htm.
Titus, Richard, Fredd Heinzelmannn, and John M. Boyle. "The Anatomy of Fraud:
Report of a Nationwide Survey." *National Institute of Justice Journal*, August 1995.
"Top Ten Investment Scams." North Carolina Division of Aging, http://
www.dhhs.state.nc.us/aging/fraud/alert22.htm (accessed April 2002).
"Travel Travesties." *AARP Bulletin*, July /August 2003.
"Twist and Shout." *AARP Bulletin*, November, 2003.
"Unholy Practices." *AARP Bulletin*, April, 2003.
"Victims of Consumer and Investment Fraud." http://www
.crimes-of-persuasion.com/Victims/victims.htm (accessed October 17, 2003).
Volz, Joe. "'Perfect Storm' for Stock Scams." *AARP Bulletin*, October 2003.
"Vote of No Confidence Major Factor in Low Crime Reporting Rates, Says National
Advocacy Group." The National Center for Victims of Crime, March 9, 2003,
http://www.nvc.org/press/releases/03093003.html.
"When the Kids Play Cupid." *AARP Magazine*, September/October 2003.
Whitlock, Charles R. *Chuck Whitlock's Scam School*. New York: MacMillan, 1997.
"Work-at-Home Scams." *AARP home*, March 5, 2004, http://www.aarp.org/
consumerprotect=frauds/Articles/a2002-10-02-FraudsWorkatHome.html.
"Work-at-Home Scams." National Consumers League's National Fraud Informa-
tion Center, http://www.fraud.org/tips/telemarketing/workathome.htm
(accessed March 5, 2004).
"The Year's Worst Consumer Horror Stories." MSN Money, November 12, 2002,
http://moneycentral.msn.com/articles/banking/basics/
10621.asp?special-msn.
Yeske, David. "Home-Equity Debt: Don't Use Your Home as a Checkbook." *Military
Officer* 1, no. 10 (October 2003).
"You Have Won a Cadillac!" North Carolina Division of Aging, April 10, 2002,
http://www.dhhs.state.nv.us/aging/fraud/alert33.htm.
Young, Nolan. "The Sweetheart Swindle." http://www.geocities.com/
s_o_s_elderabuse/TheSweetheartSwindle1999.html (accessed October 27, 2003).
——— "Q&A: Scams, Gold Diggers, and Red Flags." http://www
.aloveinrussia.com/q_n_a/scams_rf_gd.shtml (accessed November 6, 2003).
Zaslow, Jeffrey. "Unmarried with Grandchildren: Seniors Shacking Up Face Unexpected Issues." *Wall Street Journal*, March 4, 2004, D1.

Index

About the Authors

BETTY L. ALT is lecturer in sociology at Colorado State University, Pueblo. She is the co-author of *Wicked Women* (2000) and author of *Black Soldiers, White Wars* (2002).

SANDRA K. WELLS is chief investigator in the Pueblo, Colorado, District Attorney's office. She is the co-author of *Wicked Women* (2000).